UNMASKING SATAN

RICHARD MAYHUE

UNMASKING
SATAN

Though intended for personal reading
and profit, this book is part of the Victor
Adult Elective Series and therefore is also
intended for group study. A Leader's Guide
with Victor Multiuse Transparency Masters is available
from your local bookstore or from the publisher.

VICTOR BOOKS®
A DIVISION OF SCRIPTURE PRESS PUBLICATIONS INC.
USA CANADA ENGLAND

Second printing, 1988

Scripture quotations are from the *New American Standard Bible,* © the Lockman Foundation 1960, 1962, 1963, 1968, 1971, 1972, 1973, 1975, 1977. Scripture quotations marked NIV are from the *Holy Bible, New International Version,* © 1973, 1978, 1984, International Bible Society. Used by permission of Zondervan Bible Publishers.

Recommended Dewey Decimal Classification: 248.4

Suggested Subject Heading: CHRISTIAN LIVING

Library of Congress Catalog Card Number: 88-60216

ISBN: 0-89693-603-1

C O N T E N T S

For

Skeeter and Wanda Hollenbeck
Jeanine Mariscal
Chuck Raynes
Jeremiah and Edie Riffe
Bill and Lois Stallo

who loved me enough as a new believer to

- solidify my hatred of sin
- encourage my worship of God
- deepen my love for God's Word
- stimulate my passion for evangelism
- heighten my desire to be like Christ
- strengthen my commitment to the local church

F O R E W O R D

In recent years, so many books have been published about Satan and demons that I have questioned whether we need any more.

But I'm glad that at least one more has been written, the book you now hold in your hand.

Why? Because *Unmasking Satan* is a practical study that shows you how to recognize the enemy, understand his strategy, and defeat him. Dr. Mayhue is not content merely to pass along orthodox biblical theology. He shows you how to turn *learning* into *living* so that God's truth indeed becomes your shield and buckler in your warfare against the hosts of hell (Psalm 91:4).

A word of warning: if you *read* this book but fail to *apply* its practical counsel, then Satan will have won the victory. Remember, we get the blessing not just by hearing the Word, but by doing it. The enemy doesn't care how much we learn so long as we don't put it into practice.

"Satan deals in subtleties," said the late Vance Havner. "Our Lord deals in simplicities." Dr. Mayhue has explained, illustrated, and applied these profound "simplicities" in such

a practical way that even the youngest believer can understand and practice them.

I pray that God will use this "manual of arms" to bring
many of His people out of retreat and defeat and into victory.

Warren W. Wiersbe
General Director,
Back to the Bible
Lincoln, Nebraska

Wilsonian theology says, "The devil made me do it!" Comedian Flip Wilson was on the right track, because Satan is eager to influence our lives with his tricks. If Flip had only added, "But God will hold *me* personally accountable for my sin," he would have been totally on target (2 Cor. 5:10).

Having studied the schemes of Satan for many years, my point in writing is to warn you that Satan continues on his malignant rampage. Space-age Christians rank as leading candidates to become choice morsels in the mouth of the "roaring lion" (1 Peter 5:8).

Beloved radio commentator Paul Harvey pictured Satan's attack in his piece, "If I Were the Devil ... "

> *If I were the prince of darkness, I would want to engulf the whole earth in darkness.*
>
> *I'd have a third of its real estate and four-fifths of its population, but I would not be happy until I had seized the ripest apple on the tree. So I should set about whatever necessary to take over the United States.*
>
> *I would begin with a campaign of whisper. With the*

wisdom of a serpent, I would whisper, "The Bible is a myth." I would convince them that "man created God," instead of the other way around. I'd whisper that "what is bad is good and what is good is square."

In the ears of the young married I would whisper that work is debasing, that cocktail parties are good for you ...

And to the old I would teach to pray, to say after me, "Our father which art in Washington ... "

Then I'd get organized. I'd educate authors in how to make lurid literature exciting so that anything else would appear dull, uninteresting. I'd threaten TV with dirtier movies and vice versa. I'd peddle narcotics to whom I could. I'd sell alcohol to ladies and gentlemen of distinction. I'd tranquilize the rest with pills.

If I were the Devil I would encourage schools to refine young intellects, but neglect to discipline emotions, let those run wild.

I'd designate an atheist to front for me before the Highest Courts and I'd get preachers to say, "She's right." ...

With flattery and promises of power I would get the courts to vote against God in favor of pornography.

Thus I would evict God from the courthouse, from the school house, then from the House of Congress. Then in His own churches I'd substitute psychology for religion and deify science. That way men would become smart enough to control everything.

If I were Satan I'd make the symbol of Easter an egg ... and the symbol of Christmas a bottle. ...

If I were the Devil I'd take from those who have and give to those who wanted until I had killed the incentive of the ambitious. Then my police state would force everybody back to work.

Then I could separate families, putting children into

unicamps.
If I were Satan, I'd just keep on doing what I am doing and the whole world would go to Hell as sure as the Devil.'

Satan's chief objective in your life is to allow your profession of faith while preventing its daily practice. He spies out your life regularly to determine advantageous attack points.
Over 300 years ago Puritan preacher Thomas Brooks wrote to his flock about Satan. His timeless "call to arms" is classic.

Beloved in our dearest Lord,
Christ, the Scripture, your own hearts, and Satan's devices, are the four prime things that should be first and most studied and searched. If any cast off the study of these, they cannot be safe here, nor happy hereafter. It is my work as a Christian, but much more as I am a Watchman, to do my best to discover the fullness of Christ, the emptiness of the creature, and the snares of the great deceiver; which I have endeavoured to do in the following discourse, according to that measure of grace which I have received from the Lord.[2]

Heeding Brooks' warning, our thoughts concentrate primarily on Satan's devices (Eph. 6:11). For only by knowing his battle plan can we be armed with a sure knowledge of Satan's attempts on our lives.
In *The Screwtape Letters,* C.S. Lewis makes a memorable statement that draws the boundaries for our study.

There are two equal and opposite errors into which our race can fall about the devils. One is to disbelieve in their existence. The other is to believe, and to feel an excessive and unhealthy interest in them.[3]

We'll assume Satan's personal reality. At the same time, we want to study the prince of darkness neither further nor deeper than the Scriptures allow. Our goal is to become biblically equipped for spiritual conflict with the soldiers of hell.⁴ The sabre of God's Word will victoriously slash through and penetrate Satan's domain.

The Bible serves as the battle manual for God's army. It outlines by instruction and illustration the specific schemes in Satan's bag of tricks (2 Cor. 2:11). No victorious military strategist would enter battle without first poring over detailed intelligence reports on his adversary. So God has provided us with vivid descriptions of our enemy's past exploits. Ignorance can never be used to excuse defeat at Satan's hands.

Since the fall of mankind in Eden, Satan has been enlisting the human race as coconspirators against God's kingdom. He does this by influencing kingdom citizens to think differently than God thinks and thus to act differently than God would have us to live (Prov. 23:7; 27:19).

It's my purpose to expose the mind of Satan for you so that we can guard against his devious ways. *Unmasking Satan* catalogs our adversary's tricks and then relates them to practical twentieth-century living. Biblical countertactics for each of Satan's traps can be found in Scripture and are included here. With these tools we can guard against being duped by Satan, who disguises himself as an angel of light (2 Cor. 11:14).

Make no mistake about it—Satan would like nothing more than to add your "scalp" to his growing collection. But there is good news for Christians. Jesus Christ reigns as our protector and the source of our power to defeat Satan (Heb. 2:14-15). Through him we overwhelmingly conquer (Rom. 8:37; 1 Cor. 15:57).

I will lift up my eyes to the mountains;
From whence shall my help come?

My help comes from the Lord,
Who made heaven and earth.
He will not allow your foot to slip;
He who keeps you will not slumber.
Behold, He who keeps Israel
Will neither slumber nor sleep.

The Lord is your keeper;
The Lord is your shade on your right hand.
The sun will not smite you by day,
Nor the moon by night.
The Lord will protect you from all evil;
He will keep your soul.
The Lord will guard your going out and your coming in
From this time forth and forever. (Psalm 121)

1. Satan's Battle Plan

Recently an elder in our church, who captains a flight crew for a major airline, gave me this article from his company. It served as a warning to pilots. It serves as a warning to us.

THE ENEMY:

I am more powerful than the combined armies of the world. I have destroyed more men than all the wars of all nations. I massacre thousands of people every year. I am more deadly than bullets and I have wrecked more homes than tornadoes and hurricanes.

In the United States alone, I steal over $500 million each year. I spare no one, and I find victims among the rich and poor alike, the young and old, the strong and weak. Widows know me to their everlasting sorrow. I loom up in such proportions that I cast my shadow over every field of labor. I lurk in unseen places and do most of my work silently. You are warned against me, yet you heed me not. I am relentless, merciless and cruel. I am everywhere—in the home, on the streets, in the factory, at railroad crossings, on land, in the air and on the *sea.*

I bring sickness, degradation and death, yet few seek me to destroy me. I crush. I maim. I will give you nothing and I may rob you of everything you have.

I am your worst enemy—I am CARELESSNESS.[1]

As carelessness assaults the airline industry, Satan assaults the Christian. Only worse.

So Paul alerted the flock at Corinth to their chief foe. In 2 Corinthians 2:11 Paul writes out of love, "in order that no advantage be taken of us by Satan; for we are not ignorant of his schemes." Our thinking for the next few pages centers on this incredibly important truth.

Earlier in this decade the devil rated a three-page spread in *Newsweek*—"Giving the Devil His Due." It contained a survey of how American theologians and pastors in general have debunked and demythologized Satan, making him nothing more than a vestigial religious figure who has been trivialized by a thousand superstitions. Kenneth Woodward, noted religious correspondent for *Newsweek,* concluded with words the devil undoubtedly welcomed, "In these harrowing times, Satan's cleverest ploy would be to convince mankind that a pallid, personal devil really does exist."[2]

However, there are many who have testified to not only his personal reality but also his power. Christ would testify to his brutal temptation (Matt. 4:1-11). Satan prevented Paul from returning to Thessalonica (1 Thes. 2:18). The archangel Michael actually contended with him over the body of Moses (Jude 9). Peter experienced his painful sifting (Luke 22:31-32) and Adam and Eve his clever deception (Gen. 3:1-6).

Martin Luther put the truth of Satan's power to music in the first stanza of "A Mighty Fortress Is Our God." It is good theology because it agrees with God's Word on Satan.

For still our ancient foe

Doth seek to work us woe—
His craft and pow'r are great,
And, armed with cruel hate,
On earth is not his equal.

Someone once asked famed evangelist Billy Sunday, "Why do you believe in a real devil?"

He replied, "The Bible declares it to be so, and further, I have done business with him myself." By both scriptural revelation and life's reality, Sunday declared Satan to be a personal and formidable enemy.

A REAL SPIRITUAL ENEMY

Paul intended the Corinthians to nail down this truth—Satan is a very real enemy (2 Cor. 2:11). We know so by his names and nature. Satan's names communicate an unmistakable message. Don't miss it!

Names. An angel of the Lord told Joseph that his son would be called Immanuel, which means "God with us" (Matt. 1:23). "Fool" is the meaning of *Nabal*, and Nabal lived out his name (1 Sam. 25:25). In the same way, Satan's names reveal his character.

Paul uses the name *Satan* in 2 Corinthians 2:11; *Satan* means adversary or enemy. The angel who blocked Balaam's way (Num. 22:22) and the leader of an opposing faction (1 Kings 11:23) were "satans" of their day.

Satan stands as God's adversary. He opposes all that God stands for—light, holiness, and righteousness. He is also the Christian's enemy (Eph. 6:12).

Another major title is *devil.* Paul used this in Ephesians 6:11 to warn that Satan is additionally a slanderer or accuser. John reported that in heaven the devil is an accuser of Christians day and night before God (Rev. 12:10).

Think about the following other names used of Satan. If you ever doubted his capacity for evil, these will make you a

17

believer. Satan by name sounds meaner than a junkyard dog.

- Serpent (Gen. 3:14; Rev. 12:9; 20:2)
- Tempter (Matt. 4:3; 1 Thes. 3:5)
- Enemy (Matt. 13:25, 39)
- Evil one (Matt. 13:19; 1 John 2:13-14)
- Prince of demons (Mark 3:22)
- Father of lies (John 8:44)
- Murderer (John 8:44)
- Roaring lion (1 Peter 5:8)
- Deceiver (Rev. 12:9)
- Dragon (Rev. 12:7, 9; 20:2)

Nature. Jesus' testimony to the Pharisees exposes the devil's true character (John 8:44). He is both liar and murderer. He lives in contrast to Jesus who is both truth and life (John 14:6).

In the Garden of Eden, Satan first lied to Adam and Eve, "You surely shall not die" (Gen. 3:4). Following the course of Satan's dishonest direction, Adam and Eve ate from the tree of the knowledge of good and evil and experienced spiritual death in their relationship with God (2:15-17). God's warning proved to be true, while Satan's words contained a lie and his ways led to death.

Ananias and Sapphira experienced a similar encounter. Peter asked, "Ananias, why has Satan filled your heart to lie to the Holy Spirit?" (Acts 5:3) Because they lied, they died (5:5, 10). Paul reports that the human race exchanged the truth of God for the lie and worshiped and served the creation rather than the Creator (Rom. 1:25), which led to their death (Rom. 6:23).

Modern-day satanists, worshipers of Satan, don't always hide the devil's dishonest nature. Anton LaVey openly writes of nine diabolical statements in *The Satanic Bible*.[3]

Sample these statements about Satan's lying and life-taking ways.

■ Satan represents indulgence, instead of abstinence.

■ Satan represents kindness to those who deserve it, instead of love wasted on ingrates.

■ Satan represents vengeance, instead of turning the other cheek.

■ Satan represents all of the so-called sins, as they all lead to physical, mental, or emotional gratification.

Along with lying and murdering, Satan does much more. He is also identified in Scripture by these marks.

■ Master disguiser (2 Cor. 11:13-15)
■ Devourer (1 Peter 5:8)
■ Schemer (2 Cor. 2:11; Eph. 6:11)
■ Ruler of this age (John 12:31; 2 Cor. 4:4)

D.L. Moody once told a story about a pastor who was preparing a message on the importance of receiving Christ now, not later. After studying to the point of exhaustion, the preacher napped and had this enlightening dream.

He saw himself transported to hell where he overheard a conversation between several of Satan's emissaries. They were huddled together trying to devise schemes for leading people on earth into the same fate as theirs. One of the spirits said, "I'll go tell men and women that the Bible is not the Word of God and that it's not to be trusted." The others responded, "That isn't enough." Another spoke up, "I'll go tell them that God doesn't exist, that Christ was only a good man, and that there really is no heaven or hell." Again the response was negative. Finally, a third member said, "I'll go tell the people there is a God, a Saviour, a heaven, and a hell. But I'll get them to think they've got all the time in the world to be saved. I'll encourage them to put the decision off." "That's it!" the others shouted with glee. "That's what we want them to hear." And they chose him as their messenger.

Satan is both real and dangerous. His names and nature point him out as God's enemy and, therefore, the Christian's foe. Be warned—Satan lives and operates according to his character.

SATAN'S CHIEF TARGET AND ACTIVITY

The second truth Paul conveys to the Corinthians lies in the phrase, "in order that no advantage be taken of us" (2 Cor. 2:11). Satan rules as the commanding general of the opposing army. He daily attempts, as the *New International Version* puts it, to "outwit" us in spiritual warfare. Deviousness colors Satan's character.

Satan is a guerilla warrior who disguises himself at times as a friend of God (2 Cor. 11:14). To make the battle more difficult, Satan wages an invisible spiritual war using the most clever tactics ever devised. He stands committed to Luciferian espionage. He appears as a friend on the outside but inside he remains our deceiving enemy. His lying statements, garnished with truth, are poison to the soul.

Where does Satan aim his fiery darts? (Eph. 6:16) Paul gives us a clear answer in 2 Corinthians 11:3: "But I am afraid, lest as the serpent deceived Eve by his craftiness, *your minds* should be led astray from the simplicity and purity of devotion to Christ" (emphasis added).

The Greek word translated "schemes" in 2 Corinthians 2:11 and a different word also translated "schemes" in Ephesians 6:11 both refer to Satan's manipulation of the mind. Satan plays mind games with Christians. Our minds are Satan's chief target.

The Christian's thought life becomes the battlefield for spiritual conquest. The large number of statements from God on the importance of the believer's mind being spiritually strong reinforce this truth (Matt. 22:37; Rom. 12:2; 2 Cor. 4:4; 2 Cor. 10:5; Phil. 4:8; Col. 3:2; 1 Peter 1:13).

Since Satan aims at the Christian's mind, what does he

want to accomplish? Before we answer this significant question, let me review several Scriptures.

> *You have heard that it was said, "You shall not commit adultery"; but I say to you, that every one who looks on a woman to lust for her has committed adultery with her already in his heart.* (Matt. 5:27-28)

> *As in water face reflects face, so the heart of man reflects man.* (Prov. 27:19)

> *For as he thinks within himself, so he is.* (Prov. 23:7)

What we are on the inside determines who we are on the outside. Satan attempts to influence our minds so he can influence our lives. *Satan's chief activity in the lives of Christians is to cause them to think contrary to God's Word and thus act disobediently to God's will.*

Seventeenth-century Puritan preacher Thomas Watson put it this way, "This is Satan's masterpiece, if he can keep them from the belief of the truth, he is sure to keep them from the practice of it."

A GOD-EXPOSED SPIRITUAL ENEMY

Paul concludes, "We are not ignorant of his schemes" (2 Cor. 2:11). When I first read this I was tremendously relieved to know that there was hope. I wondered what book at the Christian bookstore would make me knowledgeable of Satan's schemes. Then it dawned on me—the Bible.

I had spoken at the chapel of a professional sports team in Los Angeles. I was eating breakfast with the players when one of them asked me, "How do we fight the spiritual battle?" I went on to tell him that it is much like winning a football game; you've got to have a great offense and a great defense. Athletes pore over game films of their opponents, compiling a notebook of expected plays, defensive tactics, strengths, and weaknesses. The Bible is God's game film on Satan.

Every military leader devours intelligence reports on the enemy before he enters battle. Our intelligence report on Satan is in the Bible. Ignorance of the enemy will never be a valid excuse if we lose. God has given us a decided edge in the contest with advance information on our enemy.

General George Patton of World War II fame was seldom at a loss for words. What he said during a battle in North Africa may be legend, but it typified the man. Patton's troops and tanks were engaged in a successful counterattack against German forces under General Erwin Rommel. Patton is reported to have shouted in the thick of the battle, "I read your book, Rommel! I read your book!" And that he had. In Rommel's book *Infantry Attacks*, he had carefully detailed his military strategy. And Patton, having read it and knowing what to expect, planned his moves accordingly. We who read Satan's plans in God's Book can be prepared for spiritual battle like Patton.

SATAN'S GOALS

It's important to know what Satan wants to achieve. First, Satan desires to be like God.

> But you said in your heart, "I will ascend to heaven; I will raise my throne above the stars of God, and I will sit on the mount of assembly in the recesses of the north. I will ascend above the heights of the clouds; I will make myself like the Most High." (Isa. 14:13-14)

Second, Satan desires to sit on God's throne. That's obvious from Isaiah 14:13, but it's also emphasized several other places in Scripture. Satan's devilish associate, the Antichrist, will strain to unseat Christ from His rightful kingdom throne

(Dan. 11:36-37; Matt. 24:15).

> Let no one in any way deceive you, for it will not come unless the apostasy comes first, and the man of lawlessness is revealed, the son of destruction, who opposes and exalts himself above every so-called god or object of worship, so that he takes his seat in the temple of God, displaying himself as being God. (2 Thes. 2:3-4)

Ultimately, Satan craves to be worshiped as God. He even tried to lure the Son of God.

> And he led Him up and showed Him all the kingdoms of the world in a moment of time. And the devil said to Him, "I will give You all this domain and its glory; for it has been handed over to me, and I give it to whomever I wish. Therefore if You worship before me, it shall all be Yours." And Jesus answered and said to him, "It is written, 'You shall worship the Lord your God and serve Him only.'" (Luke 4:5-8)

SATAN'S OBJECTIVES

Satan's goals will be reached by accomplishing several well-chosen objectives in the Christian's life. After ten years of reading, studying, and thinking about this, I believe Satan has four major objectives for the Christian. If he can accomplish one or more, he is moving toward his goals. It is important for you to understand these objectives, because Satan's attacks against you will be in one of these four broad areas.

First, Satan will attempt to *distort or deny the truth of God's Word.* That's how Satan tripped up Peter in Matthew 16. Jesus had earlier called Satan's bluff, however, and the devil failed in his attempt on Christ (Matt. 4).

Second, Satan will try to *discredit the testimony of God's people.* It succeeded with Ananias and Sapphira (Acts 5), and he'll try it on Christian leaders today (1 Tim. 3).

Next, by *depressing or destroying the believer's enthusiasm for God's work,* Satan will assault our souls. The roaring lion of hell tried this on both Paul (2 Cor. 12:7-10) and Peter (Luke 22:31-34).

Fourth, if Satan can *dilute the effectiveness of God's church,* he will be moving toward his goals. Both David (1 Chron. 21:1-8) and Judas (Luke 22:3-6) knew the pain inflicted with this type of attack.

For each objective, Satan has a variety of tactics or specific spiritual warfare techniques to achieve victory. I have identified over twenty tactics in the historical narratives and teaching portions of Scripture. In the following pages, we will be examining the three most potentially dangerous tactics for each of Satan's four objectives.

From a great chess player of Cincinnati, we learn that in the early part of the last century an artist who was also a great chess player painted a picture of a chess game. The players were a young man and Satan. The young man manipulated the white pieces; Satan the black pieces. The issue of the game was this: should the young man win, he was to be forever free from the power of evil; should the devil win, the young man was to be his slave forever. The artist evidently believed in the supreme power of evil, for his picture presented the devil as victor.

In the conception of the artist, the devil had just moved his queen and had announced a checkmate in four moves. The young man's hand hovered over his rook; his face paled with amazement—there was no hope. The devil wins! He was to be a slave forever.

For years, this picture hung in a great art gallery. Chess players from all over the world viewed the picture. They acquiesced in the thought of the artist. The devil wins! After several years a chess doubter arose; he studied the picture and became convinced that there was but one chess player upon the earth who could give him assurance that the artist of this picture was right in his conception of the winner. The chess player was the aged Paul Morphy, a resident of New Orleans, Louisiana. Morphy was a supreme master of chess in his day, an undefeated champion. A scheme was arranged through which Morphy was brought to Cincinnati to view the chess picture.

Morphy stood before the picture, five minutes, ten minutes, twenty minutes, thirty minutes. He was all concentration; he lifted and lowered his hands as, in imagination, he made and eliminated moves. Suddenly, his hand paused, his eyes burned with the vision of an unthought-of combination. Suddenly, he shouted, "Young man, make that move. That's the move!"

To the amazement of all, the old master, the supreme chess personality, had discovered a combination that the creating artist had not considered. The young man defeated the Devil.[4]

If we think as God thinks and avoid the schemes of Satan, Satan will not take advantage of us. When we are engaged in spiritual warfare, "checkmate" can be our response to the devil if we let the Word of God richly dwell within us (Col. 3:16).

DISTORT OR DENY THE TRUTH OF GOD'S WORD

The Historical Point of View, put briefly, means that when a learned man is presented with any statement in an ancient author, the one question he never asks is whether it is true. He asks who influenced the ancient writer, and how far the statement is consistent with what he said in other books, and what phase in the writer's development, or in the general history of thought, it illustrates, and how it affected later writers, and how often it has been misunderstood (specially by the learned man's own colleagues) and what the general course of criticism on it has been for the last ten years, and what is the "present state of the question." To regard the ancient writer as a possible source of knowledge—to anticipate that what he said could possibly modify your thoughts or your behaviour—this would be rejected as unutterably simple-minded. And since we cannot deceive the whole human race all the time, it is most important thus to cut every generation off from all the others; for where learning makes a free commerce between the ages there is always the danger that the characteristic errors of one may be corrected by the characteristic truths of another. But thanks be to Our Father and the Historical Point of View, great scholars are now as little nourished by the past as the most ignorant mechanic who holds that "history is bunk."

Screwtape to Wormwood,
in C.S. Lewis, *The Screwtape Letters,*
Macmillan, pp. 128–129.

2. *Scheme of Sensationalism*

An unknown author wrote this exaggerated but almost believable paraphrase of Matthew 4:9 as part of a hypothetical conversation between Satan and a pastor.

Just think of it; you'll have an immense 3,000 seat sanctuary, with revolving stage, wireless microphone, a mammoth combination reflecting pond—baptistry, 12 fountains (one for each apostle), 400 voice choir and youth orchestra, drive-thru healing booth, 60-foot copper steeple topped by a revolving globe and cross and neon "Love-Me" sign. You'll have book, cassette, radio, and T.V. ministries, a monthly magazine with your picture on the cover of each issue, a dial-a-miracle ministry and a fleet of 200 buses. All this will be yours if you'll just bow down and worship me in 25 words or less.

Because it touches so close to contemporary truth, what under other circumstances would bring a hearty chuckle only serves as a grim reminder of Satan's creativity and diligence. His scheme of sensationalism can easily lure us who live in the now generation and demand instant spiritual gratification.

SCHEME:	SENSATIONALISM—MATTHEW 4:1-11
SATAN'S LIE:	IMMEDIATE SUCCESS IS MORE DESIRABLE THAN SUCCESS IN GOD'S TIME AND IN GOD'S WAY.
GOD'S TRUTH:	1 CORINTHIANS 1:18-25

If we look at the passage leading into Matthew's description of the temptation of Christ, we'll see that Jesus has just been baptized by John, acclaimed as God's Son by His Heavenly Father, and anointed by the Holy Spirit (Matt. 3:13-17). Now, full of God's Spirit (Luke 4:1), He is led by the Spirit into the barren Judean wilderness.

The devil meets Him with three challenges for Jesus to disobey God's Word.

During this period of forty days and forty nights Christ fasted much as Moses (Ex. 34:28) and Elijah (1 Kings 19:8) had in earlier times. Luke implies that Satan's testing went beyond the three temptations of which we read and lasted the entire period (Luke 4:2). The three temptations we have recorded may have been Satan's final effort to dislodge Christ's faith in His Father's Word.

Three names in Matthew 4:1-11 describe our Lord's enemy. He is called Satan or adversary in verse 10 and "the tempter" in verse 3. But four times Matthew calls him "the devil" or slanderer (vv. 1, 5, 8, 11). If he can cause Christ to think differently from His Father and thus act disobediently to His Father's will, then Satan can rightfully accuse Christ and undermine His ministry. Satan attacks with fury during a time of stress, hunger, and fatigue. He will do the same to us.

Jesus' physical energy tank is near empty, and He stands vulnerable. But He is full of the Spirit, who will sustain Him during these crises. Satan throws the book at Jesus with testings in the area of priorities (4:3-4), presumption (4:5-7), and power (4:8-10).

PRIORITIES

Satan opened with the taunt, "If You are the Son of God." Satan had no doubts about Jesus' identity, but he wanted to put doubt in Christ's mind, so that He would feel as though He had to prove what God had already declared to be true (3:17).[1]

Every Jew understood that the term *Son of God* announced that Jesus was deity. That's why the Jews later sought to kill Christ—they knew He was calling God His own Father, making Himself equal with God (John 5:18). We also can expect to be challenged, for God has declared believers in Christ to be "sons of God" (Rom. 8:14) and "children of God" (Rom. 8:16; 1 John 3:1). We will be tempted to feel as though we must prove our identity.

In the midst of the rocky Judean wilderness, Satan challenged Jesus to command that the rocks turn to bread for Him to eat and thus satisfy His hunger. To have done this would have been to act independently of God, and Jesus would never do that (John 5:19; 8:28). To have succumbed here would have been as fatal as responding when the soldiers mockingly urged, "If You are the Son of God, come down from the cross" (Matt. 27:40).

It was not that Jesus couldn't perform the act, for later He would turn water into wine (John 2:1-11) and feed thousands from a few scraps of food (Matt. 14:13-21; 15:32-38). But Jesus lived by a set of priorities, and His top priority was doing the will and the work of His Father (John 4:34).

Christ drew His sword—God's Word (Eph. 6:17). "Man shall not live on bread alone, but on every word that proceeds out of the mouth of God (Matt. 4:4; Deut. 8:3). He parried the devil's blow with an unbeatable jab.

Jesus, the perfect Son, placed spiritual matters at a higher priority than physical matters. Then he waited for God to meet His hunger need rather than taking matters into His own hands. And in short order, angels came to care for His needs (Matt. 4:11).

We can guard against Satan by doing what Jesus did—using the Word of God. To do so, we must cultivate the appetite of Job, who treasured the words of God's mouth more than his necessary food (Job 23:12). The key to maintaining right spiritual priorities and to meeting the devil's challenges is to keep the Bible at the right priority.

The next time you feel as if you must prove you are a child of God by having something spectacular happen, remember that's how Satan tried to get to Jesus. It could be in any area—money, vacation, house, car, or food. Learn from Jesus, who believed that what God declared to be true did not need to be proven, just because someone, even Satan, challenged the truth.

PRESUMPTION

Satan does not easily accept defeat. So without spending much time licking his wounds, he tries again, this time with a surprising turn that he has just learned from Christ.

The devil took Jesus to the holy city of Jerusalem. There Satan took Jesus to the southeast corner of the temple wall, which has been estimated to have stood as much as 450 feet above the Kidron Valley below.[2]

"If You are the Son of God," roared Satan for a second time, "throw Yourself down." Then he added a twist of strategy by quoting three of four lines in Psalm 91:11-12.

The challenge remained the same—prove that You are who You claim to be. The test changed from *priorities* to *presumption,* and the technique included using Scripture to validate his request.

Again the test calls for an action similar to some Jesus would later take. He walked on water (Matt. 14:25-27) and calmed a raging storm (Mark 4:37-39). But at this point it was not the Father's will, and Jesus did not perform miracles on request—particularly for ill-advised motives. Satan sounds very much like the Pharisees later, when they demanded, "Teacher, we want to see a sign from You" (Matt. 12:38).

Many have accused Satan of distorting Scripture by leaving out the second line of the Psalms passage. However, his real error was in misinterpreting the lines actually quoted. Satan quoted them as though they applied to all people at all times in all situations. Satan is putting these words into the mouth of God, "Whenever you need special help for anything, I will be there to perform a miracle on request." Nothing could be further from the truth. The text is actually talking about spiritual, not physical, danger.

Jesus knew it was important to not only know what Scripture says but also what it means. Satan quoted the letter but Jesus knew its spirit. So He responds with appropriate words from God which were also given to the Jews by Moses, "You shall not tempt the Lord your God" (Deut. 6:16).

It reminds me of Christian's battle with Apollyon in John Bunyan's classic *Pilgrim's Progress*.[3]

Then Apollyon, espying his opportunity, began to come up close to Christian, and wrestling with him, gave him a dreadful fall; and with that Christian's sword flew out of his hand. Then said Apollyon: I am sure of thee now. And with that he had almost pressed him to death; so that Christian began to despair of life. But, as God would have it, while Apollyon was fetching of his last blow, thereby to make a full end of this good man, Christian nimbly reached out his hand for his sword, and caught it, saying: "Rejoice not against me, O mine enemy! when I fall, I shall arise." Mic. 7:8.

With that he gave him a deadly thrust, which made him give back, as one that had received a mortal wound. Christian perceiving that, made at him again saying, "Nay, in all these things we are more than conquerors through Him that loved us." Rom. 8:37. And with that Apollyon spread forth his dragon's wings, and sped him away, and Christian saw him no more. James 4:7.

God doesn't perform on demand. Just because something has happened to a particular person in the past is not a good reason to believe it will necessarily happen today to us. Satan is in the business of "manipulative bribing," but God doesn't engage in such bargaining.

Maybe you've never thought about this before, but the periods of God's greatest miracles were in the midst of the times of greatest disobedience by those who were there to see and receive. The Jews who were delivered from Egypt with great miracles of God turned right around and wanted more and bigger miracles. The nation of Israel thumbed their nose at God when He performed miracles through Elijah and Elisha.

What did all of Christ's miracles gain Him? The disdain and hatred of the Jewish leaders and rejection to a cross by the population. The Corinthians, who had a great deal going for them in the miraculous realm (2 Cor. 12:12), were the most carnal and disobedient of the churches with which Paul associated.

We need to be warned that God is not a spiritual genie ready to deliver at our call, not in the area of health or wealth or any other. We need rather to respond to God as Jesus did, "Yet not as I will, but as Thou wilt" (Matt. 26:39).

POWER

Satan saved the greatest test for last. A person can be measured by how much he or she will pay or give up to gain power. This time Satan took Jesus to a high mountain. Local traditions say they were the mountains overlooking Jericho. There the devil attempted to dazzle Jesus with his earthly domain and all of its glory. His offer went like this, "I will give You all this domain and its glory; for it has been handed over to me, and I give it to whomever I wish" (Luke 4:6).

The enticement came with one condition. Jesus would have to pay a supposedly modest price. "All these things will I give You, if You fall down and worship me" (Matt. 4:9).

That's a very attractive offer. Instead of waiting for God's timing, He could have the kingdom now—instant power. And besides, it would bypass the cross—painless power. It really boiled down to wearing the crown without bearing the cross.

Jesus' response was to turn to Satan, commanding, "Begone, Satan! For it is written, 'You shall worship the Lord your God, and serve Him only'" (Matt. 4:10).

God is a jealous God and will not tolerate divided spiritual affection (Deut. 6:15). Idolatry is unacceptable behavior according to God's first commandment (Ex. 20:3), and the Apostle John wrote, "Little children, guard yourselves from idols" (1 John 5:21).

Although Jesus' reign over the world's population is yet future, it was not quite true that He didn't have any power while He was on earth. He demonstrated His authority over sin (Mark 2:5), sickness (Mark 2:10-12), and demons (Mark 1:23-26). Even the mention of His name brought men to their knees (John 18:3-6). Yet He was content to rest in His Father's ways and wait until the right time.

What's your price? Could you be bribed by power to take your eyes off of God and give greater allegiance to someone or something else? If you have a price, someday you'll be tested and fail.

GOD'S WAY OF TRIUMPH

Having tasted defeat for the third time, Satan turned tail and fled. Not forever, though—only until a more opportune time

(Luke 4:13). The devil was down but not out. He would return—and he will in your life too.

Our adversary is both persistent and resilient. His retreat did not mean surrender. If he came back for a return engagement with Jesus, how much more will he with us. But don't despair; the ultimate victory is ours in Christ.

Jesus teaches four important lessons in His scuffle with the evil one. First, the most effective weapon against Satan's devious lies and schemes is the truth of God's Word. God's Word spoke the world into existence (Gen. 1:3) and is settled forever in heaven (Ps. 119:89).

Next, the promise of God is validated by Jesus. James wrote, "Submit therefore to God. Resist the devil and he will flee from you" (4:7). That's exactly how Christ handled the temptation. If it worked for Him, it will also work for us.

Third, what appears foolish to the world is wisdom in God's sight. What sounds good from the lips of Satan is foolish in God's economy. God's truth, not Satan's lies, needs to dominate our thinking. Paul explains it eloquently to the Corinthians.

For the word of the cross is to those who are perishing foolishness, but to us who are being saved it is the power of God. For it is written, "I will destroy the wisdom of the wise, and the cleverness of the clever I will set aside." Where is the wise man? Where is the scribe? Where is the debater of this age? Has not God made foolish the wisdom of the world? For since in the wisdom of God the world through its wisdom did not come to know God, God was well-pleased through the foolishness of the message preached to save those who believe. For indeed Jews ask for signs, and Greeks search for wisdom; but we preach Christ crucified, to Jews a stumbling block, and to Gentiles foolishness, but to those who are the called, both Jews and Greeks,

Christ the power of God and the wisdom of God. Because the foolishness of God is wiser than men, and the weakness of God is stronger than men. (1 Cor. 1:18-25)

Fourth, Jesus demonstrates for us the power we can have if we let God's Spirit teach us. God has taken up residence in every believer through His Spirit so that we can be empowered to walk in the ways of God and thus avoid Satan's traps (1 Cor. 6:19-20; Eph. 5:18-21). We need to submit and follow the Spirit's leading.

With the weapon of His Word and the wisdom of God, not to mention His promises and the power of His Spirit, we like Jesus Christ have been prepared by God not only to wage the war but also to win.

Let these words of Scripture encourage and equip you for the battle:

Since then we have a great high priest who has passed through the heavens, Jesus the Son of God, let us hold fast our confession. For we do not have a high priest who cannot sympathize with our weaknesses, but one who has been tempted in all things as we are, yet without sin. Let us therefore draw near with confidence to the throne of grace, that we may receive mercy and may find grace to help in time of need. (Heb. 4:14-16)

3. Scheme of Ecumenicism

When I was growing up in suburban Maryland, one of my favorite activities was to go to the National Zoo in Washington, D.C. They had everything from alligators to zebras. Of them all, the primates entertained my friends and me most, especially when we played a game called, "Monkey see, monkey do." We'd stick our tongues out and make all sorts of funny faces, and the monkeys would do their best to mimic us.

It was no surprise to me to learn that the ancient theologian Augustine called Satan *Simius Dei* or "the ape of God." Everything that God does, Satan follows with an evil imitation.

SCHEME: ECUMENICISM—REVELATION 2:9; 3:9
SATAN'S LIE: ALL SINCERE RELIGIOUS ORGANIZATIONS ARE VALID EXPRESSIONS OF THE WORSHIP OF GOD.
GOD'S TRUTH: ACTS 4:12

Daniel Defoe captures the essence of this scheme in his poem, "When He Reigns, It's Hell."[1]

Wherever God erects a house of prayer,
The Devil always builds a chapel there:
And 'twill be found upon examination
The latter has the largest congregation:
For ever since he first debauched the mind,
He made a perfect conquest of mankind.
With uniformity of service, he
Reigns with a general aristocracy.
No nonconforming sects disturb his reign,
For of his yoke, there's very few complain.
He knows the genius and inclination,
And matches proper sins for every nation,
He needs no standing army government;
He always rules us by our own consent....

When Christ wrote letters to Smyrna and Philadelphia, He commented that in their city operated "a synagogue of Satan" (Rev. 2:9; 3:9). They claimed to be places of valid worship of God by people who professed to be rightly related to God. However, Jesus said their god was actually Satan, not the true, living God.

Satan's involvement with the church needs no detailed proof. Prominent mention or warnings about the devil were made to five of the seven churches in Asia Minor. We've already heard about the synagogue of Satan in Smyrna and Philadelphia. To Pergamum, Christ wrote about Satan's throne and dwelling place (Rev. 2:13). Some residents of Thyatira learned "the deep things of Satan" (Rev. 2:24). Paul warned the Ephesians how to combat Satan (Eph. 6:11-17). Where the church is being built, there is Satan on one hand erecting his own chapel and on the other hand directing his wrecking crew to destroy the true church. Where God raises up the genuine, Satan follows with the fake.

Synagogue in Greek literally means "led together." James writes to the "synagogue" or to those who were led together

39

for the true worship of Jesus Christ (2:2). There are synagogues of God and there are synagogues of Satan.

If we are not led by God in accord with His Word, then we are being led by Satan. So it was that Jesus through John warned those believers in Smyrna and Philadelphia about a group of religious Jews who had the outward appearance of legitimacy but in fact had been led together by Satan for wicked worship. Thus they deserved the title "synagogue of Satan," for they aped the true things of God.

PRINCIPLE OF SATAN'S ECUMENICISM

John explains carefully who worships at the synagogue of Satan. They were the ones who claimed to be Jews but who in fact were not. This needs to be understood in a spiritual sense, not an ethnic sense. Paul states it clearly in Romans 2:28-29:

> *For he is not a Jew who is one outwardly; neither is circumcision that which is outward in the flesh. But he is a Jew who is one inwardly; and circumcision is that which is of the heart, by the Spirit, not by the letter; and his praise is not from men, but from God.*

A group of Jews claimed to be descended from Abraham, but Jesus accused them of finding their roots in Satan (John 8:39-44). The same theme is found in the Old Testament. Frequently God warned His people about being circumcised outwardly but not inwardly (Deut. 10:16; 30:6; Jer. 4:4). " 'Behold, the days are coming,' declares the Lord, 'that I will punish all who are circumcised and yet uncircumcised' " (Jer. 9:25).

Ignatius, an early second-century church father, wrote about this very issue to the church at Philadelphia.

But if any one propound Judaism unto you, hear him

not: for it is better to hear Christianity from a man who is circumcised than Judaism from one uncircumcised. But if either the one or the other speak not concerning Jesus Christ, I look on them as tombstones and graves of the dead, whereon are inscribed only the names of men. Shun ye therefore the wicked arts and plottings of the prince of this world, lest haply ye be crushed by his devices, and wax weak in your love.[2]

The Jews of John's day attempted to rob Christianity of its rightful claim to exclusivity and uniqueness in a personal relationship with God.

So it is today. Recently I shared in a panel discussion on a major radio talk show in Los Angeles. During the heat of our discussion on the unique claims of the Bible for Christianity, a well-educated rabbi from Beverly Hills asked me point-blank, "Do you mean to tell me that if I don't believe in Jesus Christ I will go to hell?"

While he disdained such a narrow thought, he had captured the essence of what Scripture teaches. I responded, "Let me make it very clear that I personally don't commit anyone to judgment, but God has said that Jesus Christ is the only way to have a right relationship with the Heavenly Father." I quoted John 14:6, where Jesus asserts, "I am the way, and the truth, and the life; no one comes to the Father, but through me."

Through the years, Satan has set up counterfeit religions and cults to confuse God's people and to compete for the souls of those who sincerely seek to be right with God. Satan wants to distort the clear "one way" message of Scripture. Satan excels at counterfeiting.

PROTOTYPES FOR SATAN'S ECUMENICISM
Bishop Hugh Latimer, a sixteenth-century pastor in England, described Satan's religious fervor in this manner.

Who is the most diligent bishop and prelate in all England? I will tell you: it is the devil. He is the most diligent preacher of all other; he is never out of his diocese; he is never from his curé; ye shall never find him unoccupied; he is ever in his parish. . . .[3]

Long before the synagogues of Satan in Revelation 2–3, the devil dispensed his own brand of counterfeit religion labeled as the real thing. Early on, Cain tried to substitute a lesser offering than the one God had requested. God's demand for total obedience angered Cain, who then killed his brother Abel, a true worshiper (Gen. 4:3-8).

After the Flood, the descendants of Noah said, "Come, let us build for ourselves a city, and a tower whose top will reach into heaven, and let us make for ourselves a name; lest we be scattered abroad over the face of the whole earth" (Gen. 11:4). Rather than be fruitful, multiply, and fill the earth, as God had commanded (Gen. 9:1), they decided to congregate in one location and devise their own way of worship. So God confused their language and scattered them over the whole earth (Gen. 11:9).

When the Jews had been liberated by God from Egypt and while Moses waited on Mount Sinai for the Ten Commandments, the nation became impatient. They cried out to Aaron, "Come, make us a god who will go before us" (Ex. 32:1). Aaron collapsed spiritually and led them in fashioning a gold calf and in building an altar for worship (Ex. 32:2-5).

Listen to God's response:

Then the Lord spoke to Moses, "Go down at once, for your people, whom you brought up from the land of Egypt, have corrupted themselves. They have quickly turned aside from the way which I commanded them. They have made for themselves a molten calf, and have worshiped it, and have sacrificed to it, and said, 'This is your god, O Israel, who brought you up from the land of Egypt!'" And the Lord said to Moses, "I have seen this people, and behold, they are an obstinate people. Now then let Me alone, that My anger may burn against them, and that I may destroy them; and I will make of you a great nation." (Ex. 32:7-10)

Centuries afterward, Solomon did what was evil in the sight of the Lord. His wives turned his heart to other gods and he was not wholly devoted to the Lord. He even went so far as to build places of worship to these false gods (1 Kings 11:4-8).

One generation later, Jeroboam, king of the northern tribes, fashioned two golden calves—one each for Dan and Bethel. There he led in false worship (1 Kings 12:28-33). This became the general pattern followed by all of the kings of Judah and Israel until God banished Israel to Assyria and exiled Judah to Babylon.

The Old Testament closed with Malachi confronting Israel with her false worship, and the New Testament begins with Jesus rebuking the false worship of the Pharisees. Biblical history and church history could well be summed up as the conflict between those called by God and those called by Satan. All of these examples serve as prototypes for the ecumenicism of John's time that extends in sophisticated forms to our day. Satan has been hard at work to counterfeit and confuse.

PRACTICE IN SATAN'S ECUMENICISM

Several hundred years ago David Brainerd feared that the Christian community had been lulled into accepting false religion instigated by Satan. I fear that for our generation too.

I fear you are not sufficiently aware of how much false religion there is in the world; many serious Christians and valuable ministers are too easily imposed upon by this false blaze. I fear you are not sensible of the dreadful effects and consequences of this false religion. Let me tell you, it is the devil transformed into an angel of light; it is the offspring of hell, that always springs up with every revival of religion to the injury of the cause of God while it passes current with multitudes of well-meaning people for the height of religion.[4]

Satan disguises himself as angel of light and so do his servants. As God has had His true apostles, prophets, teachers, and brethren, so Satan has produced a crop of false servants also. Don't underestimate the will of Satan to do this or his ability to deceive.

Jesus warned about false Christs who would come in His name (Matt. 24:4-5, 24). False apostles surfaced in Paul's day (2 Cor. 11:13) as did false brethren (Gal. 2:4; 2 Cor. 11:26). There were false leaders and deceived followers.

The greatest caution, however, comes in regard to false teachers and prophets. There are twelve such alerts in the New Testament. Jesus sounded the alarm (Matt. 7:15; 24:11, 24; Mark 13:22). So did Luke (Acts 13:6), Peter (2 Peter 2:1), and John (1 John 4:1). The ultimate warning comes in John's Revelation about *the* false prophet (Rev. 16:13; 19:20; 20:10). Needless to say, Satan has organized to promote false religion and undermine the truth.

Satan has formulated his own trinity, composed of himself, the beast, and the false prophet (Rev. 16:13). Satan's ministers (2 Cor. 11:15) serve in the synagogues of Satan (Rev. 2:9; 3:9). They preach a false gospel (Gal. 1:6-7; 2 Cor. 11:4), teach a system of false theology called "doctrines of demons" (1 Tim. 4:1), and officiate over a false communion (1 Cor. 10:20-21).

Our world today teems with false religions and cults. More false doctrine is taught now than ever before in history through the media. You can consult any standard work on world religions or cults to identify these groups.[5] The danger has never been greater, especially from those who call themselves Christian but are not.

Satan wants to multiply false religion in the name of God. But ecumenicism will flourish only where Christians are tolerant, indifferent, or convinced that sincerity, not truth, is the mark of the authentic church. Let me illustrate this point.

I vividly remember an article in *Moody Monthly* on Mormonism (June 1980) and the letters to the editor in response (October 1980). Keep in mind that Mormonism is one of the most clearly identified cultic imitations of Christianity.

One person wrote, "I do not like you running Mormonism down. It is unchristian to run any religion down." Another commented, "To insinuate that the dear, loving, and honorable parents who send forth their sons and daughters as missionaries are not Christians is about as unchristian as I can imagine."

Thinking like this is "ecumenical," and plays right into the hand of Satan. It is also inconsistent with the thought patterns of Jesus (Matt. 23:1-39), Paul (Acts 20:28-30), Peter (2 Peter 2:1-11), and John (1 John 4:1-3), who loved the flock enough to warn them about the spiritual dangers of false religion.

Satan's attack does not end here but rather has an ultimate purpose. Let's look ahead at a rather startling scenario.

PROSPECTS FOR SATAN'S ECUMENICISM
Satan's final religious triumph won't be reached until he achieves global dominion over the world's population. He will do this by spiritual deceit. Mark carefully these scriptural warnings about Satan's *modus operandi*.

> *For false Christs and false prophets will arise and will show great signs and wonders, so as to* mislead, *if possible, even the elect. (Matt. 24:24)*

And he deceives those who dwell on the earth because of the signs which it was given him to perform in the presence of the beast, telling those who dwell on the earth to make an image to the beast who had the wound of the sword and has come to life. (Rev. 13:14)

And the light of a lamp will not shine in you any longer; and the voice of the bridegroom and bride will not be heard in you any longer; for your merchants were the great men of the earth, because all the nations were deceived by your sorcery. (Rev. 18:23)

And when the thousand years are completed, Satan will be released from prison, and will come out to deceive the nations which are in the four corners of the earth. (Rev. 20:7-8)

The scheme of ecumenicism will grow and flourish in the future. The definition of *ecumenical* in one dictionary reads,

1: worldwide or general in extent, influence, or application 2a: of, relating to, or representing the whole of a body of churches b: promoting or teaching toward worldwide Christian unity or cooperation.[6]

Our English word *ecumenical* is from the Greek word *oikoumenē*, which means "worldwide." Religious deception on a worldwide basis perfectly describes Satan's plan.

And the great dragon was thrown down, the serpent of old who is called the devil and Satan, who deceives the whole world; he was thrown down to the earth, and his angels were thrown down with him. (Rev. 12:9)

I believe this plan will be carried out by de-emphasizing

doctrine and overemphasizing experience. If Satan can deceptively unite the religious communities ecumenically so that they are accepting of one another, it will be done by making doctrine of no importance, or at least not a point of contention. The point of unity will come not in what the people believe but in what they experience. The basis of their unity will pass from objective beliefs to subjective experience. It will be deceptive enough to even mislead genuine Christians (Matt. 24:24).

While Satan has not achieved his goal of global ecumenicism yet, that is the direction he is headed. It includes believers and unbelievers in such an attractively deceptive way that the light of Christ can at times be overshadowed by the darkness of Satan.

PROTECTION FROM SATAN'S ECUMENICISM

This whole discussion raises the questions, "How can we protect ourselves against the scheme of ecumenicism? How can we avoid being party to such a spiritual tragedy?" God does want unity in the body of Christ, but not at the expense of truth (John 17:20-21). How can we test to distinguish between the authentic and the counterfeit?

Six fundamental doctrines set Christianity apart from the imitations. If a person or group can affirm with a clear conscience these basic beliefs, then they need to be recognized as part of the body of Christ.

The *exclusive authority of Scripture* (2 Tim. 3:16-17). No other written documents or decrees by a religious organization are to be equated with the Bible. Our authority and knowledge of God and His will come from Scripture alone and not from the Bible plus some other source.

The *triunity of God* (Matt. 28:19; 2 Cor. 13:14). One God exists in three individual, separate persons (Father, Son, and Holy Spirit). They are all deity and are equal in essence.

The *deity of Jesus Christ* (John 1:1; 5:18; 10:30). In Jesus of Nazareth, born of the virgin Mary, dwells all the fulness of deity in bodily form (Col. 2:9).

The *total sinfulness of man* (2 Chron. 6:36; Rom. 3:23). Every human being is born with a sin capacity leading to sin, which needs to be divinely forgiven before that person can enter into a personal, eternal relationship with God.

Jesus Christ is the only Saviour (Acts 4:12). Only through Christ's death and resurrection can a person be delivered from sin, forgiven by God, and adopted into the eternal, heavenly family of God.

Salvation by faith alone in the Lord Jesus Christ (Rom. 10:9-13; Eph. 2:8-9). A right relationship with God is entered into exclusively by faith in Jesus Christ (who He is and what He has done) without regard for any work done by the person. Salvation is based totally on God's grace and choice.

False religion edits or deletes one or more of these six basic biblical truths. If Satan can convince us that they are not important enough to insist on, then he is well on his way to causing us to think that all sincere religious organizations involve valid forms of worship of God. The most subtle form of deception is that which looks and sounds like the real thing. Be warned that "almost true" is never good enough. We come to God totally on His terms or not at all.

Remember that not everyone's god is the true God. John wrote, "Whoever denies the Son does not have the Father; the one who confesses the Son has the Father also" (1 John 2:23). To those who reject the truth of Scripture about the Father, the Son, or the Holy Spirit, we can say as did John Wesley, "Your god is my devil." Speaking about Jesus Christ, Peter declared,

> *And there is salvation in no one else; for there is no other name under heaven that has been given among men, by which we must be saved. (Acts 4:12)*

4. *Scheme of Rationalism*[1]

Does the sun always rise in the east? Of course, we respond. Can a person sail west to east and simultaneously move from the Atlantic toward the Pacific? Logic screams, no! Our rational minds compute, No way. Really?

If you took off from Paris on a supersonic Concord jet flying west, one hour after sunset, you would see the most beautiful sunrise—in the west. Why? Because your jet traveled faster than the earth rotated; so you really caught up with the sun, allowing it to rise in the west. It's also true that if you were traveling on the Panama Canal from the Atlantic to the Pacific, you would be traveling west to east. Look at a map if you still doubt.

Our rational minds don't always see the reality of truth as God designed it. Satan will use this to his advantage at every opportunity. Even Peter fell into this mental trap.

SCHEME: RATIONALISM—MATTHEW 16:13-28
SATAN'S LIE: IT'S OK TO SUBSTITUTE HUMAN REASON FOR SIMPLE, CHILDLIKE FAITH ANCHORED IN GOD'S WORD.
GOD'S TRUTH: ISAIAH 55:8-9

During a recent Bible Q & A session on the University of California at Santa Barbara campus, a student asked about the propriety of sexual relationships during an engagement. An about-to-be married friend had justified her physical relationship before marriage by saying that because they were in love and planning to be wed, it was acceptable to God. This collegiate wanted to know if her friend's reasoning was right or wrong.

If we depended only on our own thinking, the desires of our hearts, and the course of society, then we would likely say that in that situation a sexual relationship is OK. The two were in love and planning to marry. But that's not the answer I gave. By turning to our Bibles we found the ultimate answer from God's revelation, not man's rationalization (1 Thes. 4:1-8; Heb. 13:4). Satan always wants us to substitute our thinking for God's. Every time we do, we'll be wrong.

BUILDUP

The question Jesus asked was of paramount importance. "Who do people say that the Son of man is?" (Matt. 16:13) To get this one wrong would be to miss eternal life (John 20:31). About Jesus, some guessed John the Baptist; others, Elijah. Jeremiah and one of the prophets were also included in the possibilities (Matt. 16:14).

Jesus then asked, "But who do you say that I am?" (16:15) Like a little kid in school who knows the answer and blurts it out almost before the question is over, Peter shot back, "Thou art the Christ, the Son of the living God" (16:16).

Peter's answer meant that he understood that Jesus was God incarnate; that Jesus fulfilled God's promises for another prophet (Deut. 18:18); that Jesus would deliver the nation (Ps. 2); that Jesus would be king, and better days would be ahead for Israel (Zech. 14:1-8). Peter understood that Jesus would restore the kingdom to Israel (Acts 1:6) and that in Him the Lord's glory would be revealed (Isa. 40:5). The

Christ, the Son of the living God, would fulfill these long-awaited promises of God to Israel through the prophets.

Now Jesus quickly commended Peter with a blessed building up (Matt. 16:17). Simon's source of info was God, not man. Earlier, Peter had come through when many of the disciples were departing. At that time Peter declared, "Lord, to whom shall we go? You have words of eternal life. And we have believed and have come to know that You are the Holy One of God" (John 6:68-69). But now Peter is even clearer. Jesus is Messiah.

Thus Peter would be significant in the building of Christ's assembly (Matt. 16:18). Great authority would be given by the King for Peter and others to help rule over the kingdom (16:19). What a glorious day for Peter and the disciples!

I'm sure they could have agreed with Frank Tillapaugh who said once in my hearing, "We have not succeeded in answering all of your questions. The answers we have found only serve to raise a whole new set of problems. In some ways we feel as confused as ever. But we believe we are confused on a higher level and about more important things." While the disciples might not have been on the mountaintop yet, certainly they were higher than ever before.

LETDOWN

The problem with every mountaintop experience, though, is that sooner or later we come to the valley ahead. In this case, the descent took place immediately. Someone has suggested that the most difficult time in life is after the battle is won, not in preparation nor in the skirmish itself. For afterward our guard is down, our judgment dull, and our will weighed down with the false notion of invincibility.

So it was that Jesus told the disciples "that He must go to Jerusalem, and suffer many things from the elders and chief priests and scribes, and be killed, and be raised up on the third day" (16:21).

51

Suffering, dying, and rising from the dead were not in Peter's thinking. He was thinking of how glorious Jesus' reign would be. Maybe like John and James, he contemplated who would sit at Christ's left and right hands (20:20-23).

Now it's not that the Old Testament didn't talk about this surprise feature. Peter would later acknowledge,

> *As to this salvation, the prophets who prophesied of the grace that would come to you made careful search and inquiry, seeking to know what person or time the Spirit of Christ within them was indicating as He predicted the sufferings of Christ and the glories to follow. (1 Peter 1:10-11)*

The prophets were confused. Perhaps they stumbled over God's Word to Daniel:

> *Then after the sixty-two weeks the Messiah will be cut off and have nothing, and the people of the prince who is to come will destroy the city and the sanctuary. And its end will come with a flood; even to the end there will be war; desolations are determined. (Dan. 9:26)*

Or, they may have puzzled over God's message through Isaiah:

> *He was despised and forsaken of men, a man of sorrows, and acquainted with grief; and like one from whom men hide their face, He was despised, and we did not esteem Him.*
> *Surely our griefs He Himself bore, and our sorrows He carried; yet we ourselves esteemed Him stricken, smitten of God, and afflicted. But He was pierced through for our transgressions, He was crushed for our iniquities; the chastening for our well-being fell upon Him, and by*

His scourging we are healed. All of us like sheep have gone astray, each of us has turned to his own way; but the Lord has caused the iniquity of us all to fall on Him. (Isa. 53:3-6)

Jesus unveils the centrality of the cross to Christianity. His implication? Without the cross there will be no crown. Unless Jesus is the Saviour, He cannot become sovereign head of God's kingdom.

Isaac Watts, father of American hymnody, wrote these wonderful words over 250 years ago. In them he expresses God's salvation intention in the cross.

When I survey the wondrous cross
On which the Prince of glory died,
My richest gain I count but loss,
And pour contempt on all my pride.

Forbid it, Lord, that I should boast,
Save in the death of Christ, my God;
All the vain things that charm me most—
I sacrifice them to His blood.

It seems certain in light of what follows that Peter did not have these thoughts in mind.

GOOF UP

Just as impulsively as he blurted out the answer to Christ's question, Peter reacts to Christ's announcement. With deep compassion and humble sincerity, Peter stepped in and pulled Jesus away from the group and began to rebuke Him. "God forbid it, Lord! This shall never happen to You" (Matt. 16:22).

To Peter, it didn't compute. Maybe he thought it just too far below the dignity of Messiah. It could be that Peter's love was too great to allow him to even think about the humility and disgrace involved in crucifixion. Undoubtedly, he acted on impulse and blurted out the foremost thought of the moment.

Many have called Peter the apostle with a "foot-shaped mouth." In some sense this can't be denied. But Peter was also an apostle on the move, so he could be redirected more easily than some of the others who had not yet gotten underway. In many ways, he is very much like some of us.

Peter's mistake is like mistakes often made in our own society. Consider these samples:

■ Let's legalize drugs so that associated violence will decline and the cost of law enforcement will decrease.

■ Let's make homosexuality and AIDS civil rights issues rather than moral and medical problems.

■ Let's continue to consider abortion a legal alternative so that women can exercise their rights and the world population will not grow unnecessarily fast.

■ Let's ease up on sexual morality because we live in a new age and because immorality—redefined as "new morality"—can really be helpful to many, as verified by recent scientific studies.

■ Let's enjoy the present to the fullest, without regard for the future because in all likelihood none of us will be around then.

■ Let's ease up on the punishment of convicted criminals, especially in regards to the death penalty, because there are greater opportunities for rehabilitation when the consequences of crime are lessened.

All of these sound plausible at first glance. However, if one thinks for a while and considers their logic in light of history, a different conclusion may well be reached. If time and thought don't change one's thinking, as it probably would not have Peter's, then one more element is necessary. Jesus directs Peter's attention that way.

SETDOWN

"Get behind Me, Satan! You are a stumbling block to Me; for you are not setting your mind on God's interests, but man's" (Matt. 16:23). Satan must have simultaneously whispered in Peter's ear, "Gotcha!" Satan did not succeed with the wilderness temptation (Matt. 4:11), so he now tries to destroy God's salvation plan through Peter.

The cross was a stumbling block to Jews (1 Cor. 1:23) and it became one to Peter. If Christ could just be tripped up by it, then Satan would have clear sailing to capture the world's allegiance and worship. Satan intended this to be a knockout punch, but it wasn't the only punch he had thrown.

Adam and Eve received Satan's first blow in Eden (Gen. 3:1-7). They were deceived into becoming coconspirators with Satan in rebellion against God's sovereign rule. As a result the entire human race throughout all of time has entered this life against God, not for Him (Rom. 3:23).

Then Satan tried to eliminate the human line of Christ's descendants to invalidate the covenant promises made to David (2 Sam. 7:12-14). Wicked Athaliah destroyed all of the royal offspring of Judah, the line of Christ, except Joash, whom Jehoshabeath rescued (2 Chron. 22:10-12). Messiah's future would have ended with the premature death of Joash, leaving no males to propagate Christ's line.

Israel, Messiah's nation, became the object of an attempted national genocide by Haman the Persian (Es. 3:6). An edict came forth from King Ahasuerus to annihilate the Jews (3:8-15). Later, Christ's own life came under attack early on by Herod, who ordered all infants under two years of age in Bethlehem to be slaughtered (Matt. 2:16).

Here, we've seen the attempt to keep Christ from the cross; later Satan would seek permission to sift Peter, resulting in his denial of Christ (Luke 22:31-32). Satan enters the scene again in Acts 5 and tries to destroy the early church through the lie of Ananias and Sapphira (Acts 5:1-11).

The Parable of the Wheat and Tares tells us how Satan undermines the Great Commission. The devil continually removes the sown Gospel seed from the heart before it has a chance to germinate (Matt. 13:4, 19). Later on Satan will attempt a heavenly *coup d'état* when the angelic army headed up by Michael is attacked by the demonic forces of Satan (Rev. 12:7-9).

Christ correctly understood that Satan now attempts to get to Him through His own disciple, Peter. How did Satan work? Through Peter's mind. By substituting a natural response to the cross rather than a supernatural one.[2] Peter's mind switched tracks from God's thinking to man's. He no longer allowed God to guide his thoughts but rather mentally computed on independent duty, unaware that Satan slyly and illegally had tapped into his mental machinery. In computer jargon, Satan acted as a "hacker." Peter's mental programming suffered from Satan's tampering.

As a result, Peter momentarily and unwittingly spoke on Satan's behalf rather than on the behalf of the one whom he had moments earlier proclaimed to be Messiah. So with almost identical words to those with which he dispatched Satan in the wilderness (Matt. 4:10), Christ rebukes Peter, "Get behind Me, Satan!" It's like saying, "Get out of my way" and "Scram" at the same time. Don't miss it—no matter who we are or what we have done for Christ in the past, the moment we buy into Satan's plan at any level, we can expect to be rebuked as though we were Satan himself.

PICKUP

How does one recover from such a devastating moment? Not only had Peter been duped by the devil, but he had been rebuked by God's Redeemer. Jesus explained to the disciples God's only plan as it relates to the implications of the cross for Christians (16:24-28). Christ gave Peter God's thoughts to reorient his thinking and to reprioritize his life. That's how to get up and go again—return to God's Word.

One of the prophets wrote,

"For My thoughts are not your thoughts, neither are your ways My ways," declares the Lord. "For as the heavens are higher than the earth, so are My ways higher than your ways, and My thoughts than your thoughts." (Isa. 55:8-9)

That's our safeguard against acting to benefit Satan's constant efforts to undermine God's kingdom. By consulting God's Word first, we make sure our thoughts have been amended by God's thoughts and our ways have been redirected to God's way.

Consider this story carefully. A soldier stood before Alexander the Great to face charges of treason. As the proceedings concluded, the king asked, "What is your name?" to which the defendant replied, "Alexander." The general then angrily pronounced, "You are guilty as charged. Therefore, either change your conduct or change your name. For no one can bear the name Alexander and act as you have."

How does your conduct reflect on your name? Are you bearing the name Christian with glory to God, or should you be renamed Satan like Peter? Think about it!

You, however, continue in the things you have learned and become convinced of, knowing from whom you have learned them; and that from childhood you have known the sacred writings which are able to give you the wisdom that leads to salvation through faith which is in Christ Jesus. All Scripture is inspired by God and profitable for teaching, for reproof, for correction, for training in righteousness; that the man of God may be adequate, equipped for every good work. (2 Tim. 3:14-17)

DISCREDIT THE TESTIMONY OF GOD'S PEOPLE

Orthodoxy, or right opinion, is, at best, a very slender part of religion. Though right tempers cannot subsist without right opinions, yet right opinions may subsist without right tempers. There may be a right opinion of God without either love or one right temper toward Him. Satan is proof of this.

John Wesley

5. *Scheme of Situationalism*

Bishop Warren Chandler, preaching to a large audience, related the story of Ananias and Sapphira, who told a lie to God and were struck dead. The preacher roared, "God doesn't strike people dead for lying like He used to. If He did, where would I be?" After the audience's laughter subsided he continued, "I tell you where I would be. I would be right here preaching to an empty house."[1]

From the humor of this true story, we move to the sobering and serious nature of God's holiness. Ananias and Sapphira trifled with truth and paid a price. No one since them, not even Satan, the father of lies, can be in any doubt about how highly God values honesty.

SCHEME: SITUATIONALISM—ACTS 5:1-11
SATAN'S LIE: GOD'S WORD IS FLEXIBLE ENOUGH TO BEND WHEN I JUDGE THAT THE SITUATION DEMANDS IT.
GOD'S TRUTH: PSALM 119:89

Vance Havner, alluding to the event recorded in Acts 5, commented to the effect that if today's churches really crave a first-century experience, they would need a mortuary in the basement. In a sense, true church growth would not be measured by how many were in the service but rather by how many departed alive.

Satan's second major objective of recruiting Christians as coconspirators against God's kingdom focuses on discrediting a believer's testimony. Satan wants us to travel on the highway of hypocrisy, to live differently from what we believe and teach, and thus lose our credibility.

Without a consistent track record, we are impotent hypocrites, unable to do anything significant on God's behalf; Satan has us where he wants us. I could cite many recent examples of well-known Christians who have lost their ministry and impact for God. In most cases they succumbed to sexual or material temptation. Yet God graciously allowed them to live.

I corresponded with one dear man who removed himself from a very influential place of service and retreated to a solitary location waiting for God's new direction. My heart ached for him, and I wanted to express my admiration for his acknowledgement of sin and genuine repentance.

He wrote in return, "I make no excuses for what I did. It was the act of a very tired and vulnerable man who didn't take seriously enough the fact that the enemy shoots hard and fast."

I thank God that His judgment in this case did not descend with the severity it did with Ananias and Sapphira. However, God will achieve kingdom triumph if we can learn from both history and current events. Let's deepen our commitment to live consistently, not situationally, with God's Word.

CIRCUMSTANCES

God had wonderfully blessed the early church. Thousands were being saved and a special spirit of commitment resulted. The apostles lived fearlessly and performed great miracles. Purity and righteousness characterized the first church.

Luke sketches the prominent features of the early church for us in Acts 4:32-37. His portrait includes

- Unity   4:32
- Powerful preaching   4:33
- Abundant grace   4:33
- Selflessness   4:34, 36-37
- Trustworthy leadership   4:35

Sin had not yet crept in to tarnish and corrode. Hypocrisy had not yet applied the brakes to kingdom advance and church building. As Genesis 1–2 paints the pristine picture of creation unflawed by sin, so Acts 1–4 portrays the church in all her blemish-free glory. But as Genesis 3 tells how sin entered the human race, Acts 5 gives the account of the first day of extreme unholy behavior in the church.

Joseph, better known as Barnabas (4:36-37), stands in contrast to Ananias and Sapphira (5:1-2). Barnabas sold a piece of land and gave all the proceeds to help those who had less than he did; he lived up to his name, "son of encouragement." Likewise, Ananias and Sapphira liquidated a piece of real estate, but under the pretense of giving it all to the church, they donated only a portion of the sale price. Spiritually speaking, Ananias did not live up to the meaning of his name—"God is grace," nor Sapphira hers—"Beautiful." Their scandal corrupted the wonder of sacrificial giving in the church.

Little did Ananias and Sapphira guess that Satan liked to target couples. Adam and Eve plus Mr. and Mrs. Job had been in the cross hairs of Satan's sight. Had either Ananias or Sapphira been strong enough to put a halt to their plan of personal glory and private riches, then the victory experienced by Job would have been theirs too. As it turned out, family tragedy resulted, much as it did to Achan's clan in earlier times when they tried to play loose with God's instructions (Josh. 7:1-26).

CONFRONTATION

Little could anyone guess that what started so well could end so tragically. The last thing Ananias expected as he laid money at the apostles' feet was a rebuke. Ananias had lied to God the Holy Spirit (Acts 5:3-4). It's one thing to lie to a man and quite another to lie to God. So Ananias got an earful.

Each person of the Godhead manifests truth as part of His divine character. The Father is the God of truth (Ps. 31:5). Jesus proclaimed Himself to be "the truth" (John 14:6). God's Holy Spirit is "the Spirit of Truth" (John 14:17; 15:26) who guides us into all truth. Ananias and Sapphira had rejected God's leading and thumbed their noses at His truth.

Since God is truth and He wants us to be like Him, it is no surprise that He wants us to walk in truth (3 John 4). It is expressed in the ninth commandment of the Mosaic Law, "You shall not bear false witness against your neighbor" (Ex. 20:16). God hates a lying tongue and a false witness (Prov. 6:16-19). That's why Paul commands the Ephesians, "Laying aside falsehood, speak truth, each one of you, with his neighbor, for we are members of one another" (Eph. 4:25).

What was the problem with Ananias and Sapphira? It wasn't that they held onto the land or even that they needed to sell. The land was theirs. God did not demand that the entire sale price be given. Rather, they lied by saying that their gift included the total sale price, when in fact they kept back some for themselves.

Satan and Ananias became teammates in lying to God. Satan filled his heart to lie (5:3) and Ananias conceived in his own heart to commit this sinful deed (5:4). All of this occurred with Sapphira's full knowledge and approval (5:2). We don't know all of the circumstances. It could be that the couple promised God they would give it all and they gave only a portion. It could be they violated Solomon's warning:

When you make a vow to God, do not be late in paying

it, for He takes no delight in fools. Pay what you vow! It is better that you should not vow than that you should vow and not pay. (Ecc. 5:4-5)

They also may have told the apostles and perhaps others that they gave it all. It could even have been with understandable reasons that they did what they did—perhaps an emergency came up, and they kept back some cash to handle it. Maybe they figured they could earn more money for God by keeping some and reinvesting it for an even greater return. I'm sure they thought they had a good reason.

Whatever their thinking, they succumbed to the scheme of situationalism. They believed that God's Word on truth and lying was flexible enough to bend when they judged the circumstances right. With this kind of thinking, perversion becomes an alternative lifestyle; pornography becomes sexual realism; permissiveness becomes sexual freedom; premarital sex becomes a loving experience; prostitution becomes surrogate reality; and lies become liberating ideas.

I recall a humorous incident in which one engine of a jet flamed out, and the plane lurched to that side. So frightened was one passenger that he muttered out loud, "God, if You get me back on the ground safely, I will give You half of my possessions." It just so happened that a pastor seated next to him overheard his promise. After the plane landed safely, the pastor said to the man, "Sir, I'm a representative of God and I'm here to collect on your promise." The passenger replied, "After we landed, I made a new promise to God. I told Him if I was ever dumb enough to get on a plane again, I would give Him all I own." Shades of Ananias and Sapphira.

CONSEQUENCES

God's judgment came swiftly. Ananias died on the spot, and everyone else wondered if they were going to join him. God's patience and mercy did not give Ananias a second chance in this instance. He became an example to the early church of what it is like to fall into the hands of the living God (Heb. 10:31).

Why was God so harsh? Why is He not so harsh with unbelievers who lie? Peter tells us that judgment begins first with the household of God (1 Peter 4:17). That's why Ananias died. He joined the ranks of Nadab and Abihu (Lev. 10:1-2), the woodcutter who worked on the Sabbath (Num. 15:32-36), and Uzzah who touched the ark (2 Sam. 6:6-7)—all believers who tried to bend the truth.

Paul warned the Corinthians that because they profaned the Lord's table, some were weak and sick and a number "slept," meaning that they died by God's hand of judgment (1 Cor. 11:29-30). John alerts us to the sobering fact that sin can lead to physical death (1 John 5:16).

You might be asking, "Were they Christians?" While only God knows for sure, there are several compelling reasons to believe that Ananias and Sapphira had trusted in Christ unto eternal life. There is no hint that they were anything else but a part of "the congregation of those who believed" (Acts 4:32). Lying to the Holy Spirit is best understood as something that Christians would do totally out of character with their new nature in Christ. This seems to be God's hand of judgment on two believers to forever remind His spiritual family how highly He values truth.

CONSISTENCY

Where Sapphira was during all of this we don't know. But three hours later she walked in and Peter sang the same song, second stanza. Sapphira met the identical end as her husband (5:9-11).

Look at Peter's question, "Why is that you have agreed *together* to put the Spirit of the Lord to the test?" (5:9) Two of God's warning systems had been violated. First, the indwelling Holy Spirit had been overriden. God's alert system had been purposely disabled and bypassed. Just as this can lead to a physical disaster on an airplane, so it can lead to spiritual disaster. "Or do you not know that your body is a temple of the Holy Spirit who is in you, whom you have from God, and that you are not your own? For you have been bought with a price: therefore glorify God in your body" (1 Cor. 6:19-20).

Second, as two Christians, Ananias and Sapphira should have exhorted one another to obey rather than turn away. That's why we all need someone to whom we are accountable. In their case, even this safeguard didn't work. Thomas Watson may have captured the point of failure in these memorable lines, "The devil would paint sin with the vermilion colour of pleasure and profit, that he may make it look fair; but I shall pull off the paint that you may see its ugly face."[2] Neither one of them exposed lying's gross features for the other.

Undoubtedly, this devil-deceived couple misread the despicable appearance of lying, which for a fatal moment caught them with its false beauty. One moment of sinful pleasure brought to an end the usefulness of Ananias and Sapphira to God's kingdom cause.

CONSIDERATIONS

Where did Ananias and Sapphira go wrong? What can we learn from them? I happen to believe that at one time they professed an unbending allegiance to God's Word. They were probably willing to die for their faith or at least be imprisoned. Somewhere they slipped. Slowly but surely they left their first love and retreated from their first works.

First, it's clear that this couple had failed to stimulate each other to love and good deeds.

Let us hold fast the confession of our hope without wavering, for He who promised is faithful; and let us consider how to stimulate one another to love and good deeds, not forsaking our own assembling together, as is the habit of some, but encouraging one another; and all the more, as you see the day drawing near. (Heb. 10:23-25)

If this special passage is true for the body of Christ, how much more for a husband and wife. How are you doing in your marriage or special relationship with another believer? Are you accountable? Do you serve as a spiritual sounding board? Do you love enough to confront? Are you courageous enough to let someone else in on the innermost secrets of your heart?

Ananias and Sapphira must also have believed that the end justified the means. This kind of thinking predates Joseph Fletcher's situational ethics. It says, "There is a lot to be gained. No one will know or get hurt. Besides, we'll do it just this one time. It won't make any difference." But it made a difference to God and eventually to Ananias and Sapphira.

In addition, the idea must have lodged in their thinking that happiness is a higher priority than holiness. That's the way the world thinks; we understand why, but Christian holiness should be our consuming passion. Jack Eckhardt, a successful businessman in Florida, received the free gift of eternal life in Jesus Christ through the ministry of Chuck Colson in the early '80s. Colson tells this story about Christianity's impact on Eckhardt's life.

One day he walked into one of his seventeen hundred Eckhardt Drug Stores—the second largest drug chain in America—and saw Playboy and Penthouse on the counters and he said, "Take those out of my drugstores." And that began a sequence of events which resulted in Playboy and Penthouse being removed from twelve thousand drugstores and retail outlets across

America because the pressure began when it came out of Eckhardt Drugs. What I like best about that story is that when I called Jack and asked, "Did you do that because you became a Christian?" he said, "Why else would I give away three million dollars? God wouldn't let me off the hook." That's the greatest definition of the lordship of Jesus Christ I've ever heard. There's a case of a man who took his stand, who had the courage to do so. He is to me one of the genuine heroes, one of the genuine conversions, because his story touches businessmen all across this country, the man who said, "God wouldn't let me off the hook."[3]

How is it with your ethics, my Christian friend? Are you centered on the path of righteousness? Or have you taken a moral or ethical detour? Let me help you check yourself out. Answer yes or no to each of these questions,

- Do you pray in public but not in private?
- Do you carry a Bible but rarely read it?
- Do you attend worship but never participate?
- Do you sing the hymns but never live them out?
- Do you talk about religion but never tell anyone about Jesus Christ?
- Do you make a big deal about giving and then give God second best?
- Do you fudge on your income tax forms?
- Have you ever been less than completely honest when filling out an employment application?
- Do you give your employer less than the kind of excellent work that you would give Christ?
- Do you go places where you don't want others to go or know you go?
- Do you watch TV and movies that wouldn't be appropriate if Christ were watching with you?
- Do you entertain thoughts that you would be ashamed

69

for others to know?

Wherever you answered yes to those questions, you are living a lie. We, like Ananias and Sapphira, deserve to die. Thank God for His mercy that spares us! Praise the Lord for His love by which He cares for us! Hallelujah for God's grace because through it He saves us!

The wisdom of Proverbs presents us with a fabulous prayer. I find myself uttering it often.

> *Two things I asked of Thee, do not refuse me before I die: Keep deception and lies far from me, give me neither poverty nor riches; feed me with the food that is my portion, lest I be full and deny Thee and say, "Who is the Lord?" Or lest I be in want and steal, and profane the name of my God. (Prov. 30:7-9)*

Whenever you are on the verge of bending the unbendable, remember, "Forever, O Lord, Thy Word is settled in heaven" (Ps. 119:89). Spend your energies living under it not trying to escape from it.

We would do well to pray with the cadets at the U.S. Military Academy at West Point:

> *Make us choose the harder right instead of the easier wrong, and never to be contented with half truth when whole truth can be won. Endow us with courage that is born of loyalty to all that is noble and worthy, that scorns to compromise with vice and injustice and knows no fear when right and truth are in jeopardy.*[4]

6. *Scheme of Individualism*

The day after preaching this material to our flock in Long Beach, a woman called to thank me for its biblical relevance. Sexual temptation had become intensely real to her. She confessed to this kind of attraction while admitting the shock that it could happen to her since she had become a Christian many years before and was very active ministering in our church.

She faced the stark reality that when a godly husband neglects or ignores a godly wife, Satan sees the crack and inserts his wedge of temptation. As the division between husband and wife widens, it will take them further than they want to go, keep them longer than they want to stay, and cost them more than they want to pay.

Paul warns us about this ever-present danger in our sex-crazed society and supplies a solution to protect us from Satan's powerful attack.

SCHEME: INDIVIDUALISM—1 CORINTHIANS 7:1-5
SATAN'S LIE: THE CHIEF MARRIAGE RESPONSIBILITY IS TO SATISFY ONESELF, NOT

ONE'S PARTNER.

GOD'S TRUTH: EPHESIANS 5:22-25

Since modern Southern California so closely resembles ancient Corinth, Chuck Swindoll has suggested that 1 Corinthians be retitled 1 Californians. The mere mention of Corinth in ancient days instantly turned one's mind to sexual immorality. The temple of Aphrodite, Greek goddess of love, was stocked with 1,000 "sacred" prostitutes. The most prominent place of pagan worship atop the Acrocorinth offered more sexual immorality than spiritual purity.

The Corinthians to whom Paul wrote had been saved out of this background and continued to live in this culture. Some of their society's promiscuity had even invaded the church (1 Cor. 5:1-13; 6:15-20). This background helps set the scene for Paul's words in 1 Corinthians 7:1-5.

THE PRINCIPLE

Apparently the Corinthians had earlier written Paul with several questions (7:1). We have Paul's responses but not the Corinthians' letter, so we must guess what the queries might have been.

Paul had most likely taught them, "It is good for a man not to touch a woman," and they were confused in its application to married couples. The word translated "touch" in this sexual context means to touch with the idea of inflaming passion. The Greek translation of the Old Testament used this word at times in reference to immorality (Gen. 20:6; Ruth 2:9; Prov. 6:29).

Paul focuses here on abstinence, not celibacy.[1] The sexual problems Paul addresses were not to be solved by staying unmarried but rather by remaining pure if single or by pursuing one's conjugal responsibilities if married. Paul certainly did not teach them celibacy since he later condemns this practice as a doctrine of demons (1 Tim. 4:1-3).

In all likelihood their question was something like, "Are

72

married couples to continue normal physical relationships after conversion?" Put another way, the Corinthians' question was, "If sexual activity outside of marriage is wrong, is sexual activity within marriage also wrong?" The Corinthians had a reputation for living at the extremes. On one hand they tolerated incest and on the other they were ready to practice sexual abstinence in marriage. Society and their own preconversion experiences with sex had left them totally confused.

I don't believe this confusion originated in Corinth but rather at the fall of humanity. God created Adam and Eve as sexual beings—male and female. It was not until they ate from the tree of the knowledge of good and evil that they noticed their nakedness and felt the need to cover up. When their spiritual intimacy with God was shattered by sin, their perfect sexual intimacy crumbled also because they had knowledge about the evil side of sex. Ever since, the human race has been confused about the relationship of spirituality and sexuality.

Some of the Corinthians struggled with the rightness of sex within marriage, since it was wrong outside of marriage. Paul had taught them this general rule, "It is good for a man not to touch a woman." Of the approximately 2.5 billion females alive today, it is good for me not to "touch" any of them—except my wife. The Corinthians had not taken this exception into consideration.

THE PROBLEM

Immorality remained a problem to married Christians couples in Corinth (7:2). One partner in a couple might believe that sex was unimportant or unspiritual. The other had to seek sexual relief outside of the marriage and thus commit adultery.

God did not create us as sexual beings for immorality but rather to experience the sublime expression of physical love between a husband and wife. God intended sex to be sacred. Marriage is designed for partnership (Gen. 2:18), procreation (Gen. 1:28), and sexual pleasure (Prov. 5:18-19). Here Paul tells how a right sexual relationship in marriage is designed also to protect the purity of husband and wife.

I certainly don't want to become Dr. Ruth of the Christian community. But it is important to address these issues, because God does in the Bible and because the situation in our society demands it. There are three basic rules that will help you avoid immorality. I tell high schoolers and college students that if they can answer yes to all three of these questions, they can have all the sex they want.

1. Is it between a man and a woman?
2. Is it after marriage, not before?
3. Is it for the gratification of your marriage partner?

These questions embrace all that God says about sex. If you can answer yes to all three, then God will bless your sexual union. If you can't answer yes to all three, then you need to abstain from sexual relationships because it is immoral and sins against God.

THE PRACTICE

To further help married couples, Paul provides three truths that should govern the sexual relationship between a husband and wife. Notice that in each case Paul applies these principles equally to the husband and wife. Each is a two-sided coin.

Exclusivity: "Let each man have his own wife and let each woman have her own husband" (7:2). *Have* is used in the sense of sexual intercourse. Paul here succinctly states the one exception to his general rule, "It is good for a man not to touch a woman." All other human beings are off limits. But it is right, not wrong, for a husband to have his own wife and a wife her own husband. Each is to be the other's exclusive sexual partner.

Responsibility: "Let the husband fulfill his duty to his wife, and likewise the wife to her husband" (7:3). Each has an obligation to satisfy the other sexually. The responsibility of the husband is to gratify the wife, not himself. Likewise, the wife is to gratify her husband, not herself. You can see that when this is the aim of both, great satisfaction will result. (Let me add that for this reason I don't normally recommend that couples with troubled marriages live apart, except under the most troubled circumstances. It is difficult to fulfill marital obligations when living in separate locations. To live separately invites great temptation.)

Authority: "The wife does not have authority over her own body, but the husband does; and likewise also the husband does not have authority over his own body, but the wife does" (7:4). Much has been written about mutual submission. Sexual authority is exercised in the spirit of Ephesians 5:21, "Be subject to one another in the fear of Christ."

If you are not experiencing a fulfilling sexual relationship in your marriage, may I suggest this solution. Sit down with your partner and be honest about the situation. Let him or her know that there is a problem. Review these three principles—exclusivity, responsibility, and authority. Make sure you practice all three and, if not, start today.

THE PROHIBITION

Paul now commands what we've seen coming all along. "Stop depriving one another" (7:5). Whether it is for so-called spiritual reasons (like the Corinthians), or out of indifference, or out of preoccupation with another area of life, or out of retaliation, stop withholding sexual gratification from your marriage partner. It could drive them to immorality.

That raises the question, "Are there any exceptions (apart from the obvious of being physically unable)?" Just one—and Paul gives the particulars. On rare occasions temporary sexual abstinence has been commanded by God. For example, when God was to appear before the nation at Sinai they were to abstain from sexual relations (Ex. 19:9-15).

Paul sets down three rules that should govern this one legitimate reason for abstinence. First, it is to be by mutual agreement. Husband and wife should talk about it ahead of time. Second, it is to be "for a time," which means a short time, not a long time. Third, the purpose is to allow each partner to focus on God in prayer.

I once read about a husband and wife who returned home from a romantic night out. After preparing for bed the husband brought his wife three aspirins and a glass of water saying, "I thought you might need these." She responded, "Thank you anyway, Honey, but I don't have a headache." Relieved, the husband blurted out, "Gotcha!" Headaches are out and prayer is in if you want to abstain.

Paul's point is clear. Our sexual responsibility goes beyond personal convenience. We are to seek to please our spouses, not ourselves. Even when the one exception to the rule is applied, the couple is to break their sexual fast by coming together again.

THE PROVOCATION

Paul then tells us why (7:5). The roaring lion is looking to discredit your Christian testimony through sexual temptation. If he can turn one partner's desire up and the other's off, he has created an ideal environment for immorality to rear its ugly head.

This poem, written around 1885, poignantly expresses some of what one neglected wife experienced.

AN UNFAITHFUL WIFE TO HER HUSBAND
Branded and blackened by my own misdeeds
I stand before you; not as one who pleads
For mercy or forgiveness, but as one,
After a wrong is done,

Who seeks the why and wherefore.
                                        Go with me,
Back to those early years of love, and see
Just where our paths diverged. You must recall
Your wild pursuit of me, outstripping all
Competitors and rivals, till at last
You bound me sure and fast
With vow and ring.
I was the central thing
In all the Universe for you just then.
Just then for me, there were no other men.
I cared
Only for tasks and pleasures that you shared.
Such happy, happy days. You wearied first.
I will not say you wearied, but a thirst
For conquest and achievement in man's realm
Left love's barque with no pilot at the helm.
The money madness, and the keen desire
To outstrip others, set your heart on fire.
Into the growing conflagration went
Romance and sentiment.
Abroad you were a man of parts and power—
Your double dower
Of brawn and brains gave you a leader's place;
At home you were dull, tired, and commonplace.
You housed me, fed me, clothed me; you were kind;
But oh, so blind, so blind.
You could not, would not, see my woman's need
Of small attentions; and you gave no heed
When I complained of loneliness; you said
"A man must think about his daily bread
And not waste time in empty social life—
He leaves that sort of duty to his wife
And pays her bills, and lets her have her way,
And feels she should be satisfied."

                                    Each day
Our lives that had been one life at the start,
Farther and farther seemed to drift apart.
Dead was the old romance of man and maid.
Your talk was all of politics or trade.
Your work, your club, the mad pursuit of gold
Absorbed your thoughts. Your duty kiss fell cold
Upon my lips. Life lost its zest, its thrill,
                                    Until
One fateful day when earth seemed very dull
It suddenly grew bright and beautiful.
I spoke a little, and he listened much;
There was attention in his eyes, and such
A note of comradeship in his low tone,
I felt no more alone.
There was a kindly interest in his air;
He spoke about the way I dressed my hair.
And praised the gown I wore.
It seemed a thousand, thousand years and more
Since I had been so noticed. Had mine ear
Been used to compliments year after year,
If I had heard you speak
As this man spoke, I had not been so weak.
The innocent beginning
Of all my sinning
Was just the woman's craving to be brought
Into the inner shrine of some man's thought.
You held me there, as sweetheart and as bride;
And then as wife, you left me far outside.
So far, so far, you could not hear me call;
You might, you should, have saved me from my fall.
I was not bad, just lonely, that was all.
A man should offer something to replace
The sweet adventure of the lover's chase
Which ends with marriage. Love's neglected laws

Pave pathways for the "Statutory Cause."[2]

By whatever means—your sexual experience before marriage, your sexual experience in marriage, your sexual fantasies, your sexual appetite—Satan will tempt you to intimacy outside of marriage. Judah, Samson, David, Solomon, and many well-known people in our day can testify that when marriage becomes unsatisfying, the temptation is to look elsewhere for sexual fulfillment.

If the old adage "The best defense is a good offense" is true, then the best defense against immorality is for each partner to be more concerned with gratifying the other than himself or herself. When pleasing each other becomes the central focus for a couple, then Satan's temptation will be rejected and sexual expectations can be fulfilled.

When wives submit to their husbands as to Christ (Eph. 5:22) and when husbands love their wives as Christ loved the church (Eph. 5:25), then the one-flesh union between husband and wife will be at its strongest. Satan will be locked out of your home and your marriage will be secure.

POSTSCRIPT
What about the single person? If a good sex life between husband and wife will protect them from temptation, what about the person who has no spouse?

Paul writes that if singles do not have self-control, they should marry (7:9). For some, sexual fulfillment is of little or no importance. This was true for Paul, who was happy remaining single (7:7). But if sexual fulfillment is important to you and a growing pressure, that is God's way of saying that you are designed for marriage. Until marriage, you are to practice self-control and live out Paul's admonition to abstain from sexual immorality and control your own body in sanctification and honor (1 Thes. 4:3-4). Joseph, handsome young man that he was, proved it can be done (Gen. 39:7-10).

79

Whether you're unmarried or married, the choice is yours. You can select God's best of purity or sample Satan's bait of immorality and be hooked by sin.

Let marriage be held in honor among all, and let the marriage bed be undefiled; for fornicators and adulterers God will judge. (Heb. 13:4)

7. *Scheme of Isolationism*

It only took some string, a little food like cereal or peanuts, a four- to six-inch stick, and a rectangular, wooden fruit box about nine inches deep. I would tie the string (ten to twenty feet long) to the stick and prop the box up with the stick. After trailing food along to its destination underneath the box, I would hide behind a bush with abundant optimism that an unsuspecting bird or rabbit (hungry and foolish enough to follow the trail) would walk underneath the box.

Then I would deliver the *coup de grace* by pulling the string to topple the stick and drop the box on top of my unwary, distracted prey. This suburban "big game hunt" consumed many of my childhood hours.

In the same way Satan is a hunter of people's souls. The more visible in God's kingdom economy, the more desirable to the devil's taste. In just the same way, a Christian feeding on the flesh rather than on God's Spirit will be trapped by Satan's bait-stick trick.

SCHEME: ISOLATIONISM—1 TIMOTHY 3:7
SATAN'S LIE: A CHRISTIAN'S REPUTATION WILL

NOT AFFECT ANYONE BUT HIM OR HER.

GOD'S TRUTH: 1 TIMOTHY 6:1

The intelligence-military community uses the acronym SMICE to describe the baits used most effectively on members of the diplomatic corps or armed forces to induce a treasonous act.[1] SMICE stands for Sex, Money, Ideology, Compromise, and Ego. Interestingly, SMICE works equally well with men in the ministry—it's just a different kind of warfare—spiritual rather than earthly. Satan has been highly successful of late with regard to spiritual treason and compromise of the heavenly citizenship.

When the devil's success rate goes up, the pastor's stock in the eyes of the community goes down. In a recent survey, 1,000 corporate executives were asked to name their most trusted confidant when faced with an ethical problem.[2] Only 1 percent said they would consult a pastor. Shocking! I'm sure that there are many reasons for ignoring those who supposedly represent God, but I do know that a large part of it is explained by the "integrity gap" in the ministry.

Psychology Today published the results of the ranking of 100 professions according to their level of respectability, desirability, and prestige.[3] Pastors ranked 52nd, just below manufacturing foremen and just ahead of power station operators. Why? Perceived lack of credibility in the community. Although hypocrisy abounds, there is no room for pastors who are financially irresponsible, sensually stalking women, halfhearted in the ministry, empire builders, glory seekers, or money-grubbers.

OBLIGATION

It's no wonder then that Paul wrote, when speaking of qualification for the ministry, "He *must* also have a good reputation with outsiders, so that he will not fall into disgrace and into the devil's trap" (1 Tim. 3:7, NIV, emphasis added).

Paul teaches that a man's worthiness for ministry rests on two factors—man's desire (1 Tim. 3:1) and God's demands (3:2-7). When both are present and test positive (3:10), then and only then is a man qualified. God's demands are not to be met with spiritual IOUs but rather delivered on a "cash and carry" basis.

God's requirements focus on three areas of a man's life—his character (3:2-3), his conduct (3:4-7), and his capabilities to lead and feed (Titus 1:9). His conduct is tested in three areas—his home (1 Tim. 3:4-5), his ministry (3:6), and his community (3:7). Each is vital for credibility and thus effectiveness in ministry. Elders are to feed people God's Word and then lead them in living it out. Unless they can live it out themselves first, they can have no hope of helping others.

It's an absolute requisite, never optional, for Christ's ambassador to have a good reputation in the community, to be known by his integrity, and to be the model of trustworthiness (2 Cor. 5:20).

But just as we have been approved by God to be entrusted with the Gospel, so we speak, not as pleasing men but God, who examines our hearts. For we never came with flattering speech, as you know, nor with a pretext for greed—God is witness—nor did we seek glory from men, either from you or from others, even though as apostles of Christ we might have asserted our authority. But we proved to be gentle among you, as a nursing mother tenderly cares for her own children. (1 Thes. 2:4-7)

That kind of ministry will foil Satan's stick trick every time.

OUTWARD LIFE

Robert Murray McCheyne is quoted as having written, "What a man is in secret, in their private duties, that he is in the eyes of God and no more."[4] While a man is not to flaunt his private life with God before men for the gain of reputation, what a man experiences in private will be revealed in public. The inward life directs the outward.

Paul says a man is to literally "have a *good witness*." His life is to precede his license to minister. That's the way it worked out early on in church history. "But select from among you, brethren, seven men of *good reputation*, full of the Spirit and of wisdom, whom we may put in charge of this task" (Acts 6:3, emphasis added). You had to have a good reputation just to wait on tables in Christ's church. Just think how that would spiritually revolutionize the church.

Widows didn't automatically qualify for help from the church just because their husbands had died. Unless they matched up with several qualifications, they could not be on the widows' list. One of the marks they looked for was "a reputation for good works" (1 Tim. 5:10). So how one lived had a major impact on how one related to the church, the community, and the testings of Satan.

Being a *witness* was an important feature of the early church. On at least twenty occasions, Luke writes of the concept. Here's a sample (emphasis added).

It is therefore necessary that of the men who have accompanied us all the time that the Lord Jesus went in and out among us—beginning with the baptism of John, until the day that He was taken up from us—one of these should become a witness *with us of His resurrection. (Acts 1:21-22)*

This Jesus God raised up again, to which we are all witnesses. *(Acts 2:32)*

But you disowned the Holy and Righteous One, and asked for a murderer to be granted to you, but put to death the Prince of life, the One whom God raised from the dead, a fact to which we are witnesses. *(Acts 3:14-15)*

And with great power the apostles were giving witness *to the resurrection of the Lord Jesus, and abundant grace was upon them all. (Acts 4:33)*

Three basic ideas inherently attach themselves to the witness activity.

1. A witness has an assured, confirmed testimony.
2. A witness does not change his testimony when pressured by people or circumstances.
3. A witness does not perjure the reliability of his testimony by a contradictory lifestyle.

Satan would love nothing more than a "bad" witness. In so doing, the leader's effectiveness factor in spiritual matters sinks like a cement-filled submarine. Lifestyles that don't match ministry message suffer the ignoble fruits of spiritual impotence, and the devil chalks up another mark for his side. As one man put it, "Show me how the Resurrection changed your life before you try to convince me that the Resurrection is true."

OUTSIDERS

Who are the *outsiders?* Are they Christians in another congregation or people outside of God's spiritual family? Paul has unbelievers in mind here as elsewhere in Scripture.

Conduct yourselves with wisdom toward outsiders, making the most of the opportunity. (Col. 4:5)

For what have I to do with judging outsiders? Do you not judge those who are within the church? But those who are outside, God judges. Remove the wicked man from among yourselves. (1 Cor. 5:12-13)

Why such a big deal? Because hypocrisy in the ranks of Christian leaders has been one of the biggest barriers to people's reaching the cross. As a teenager I signed out of church because of rampant hypocrisy, while being blind to my own of a different nature. Integrity serves powerfully to authenticate Gospel preaching.

One dictionary defines *integrity* as "the quality or state of being complete or undivided."[5] We live in a world that desperately needs integrity but finds it in few quarters.

Billy Graham, aware of the church's plight, recently commented on the simple epitaph he would like to leave as a reminder of his ministry. It would read, "A sinner saved by grace; a man who, like the Psalmist, walked in his integrity."[6]

The only way to bring people into the kingdom of God and out of Satan's dark domain is to demonstrate that the Gospel does make a difference; it can make a broken person whole, complete, and undivided. Our reputations within ourselves and within the church are not enough. Our lives must be consistent with our message if we are to effectively touch people with Christ's message of eternal life.

OUTCOME

For the unwary and unthinking Christian, Satan has two surprises waiting. When the string pulls the stick away and the box drops, the devil's snare effectively results in reproach. Its a two-step approach—first the snare, then the reproach.

Diabolos, or *devil,* is used here to describe Satan as a slanderer. Much as he did to Israel (Zech. 3:1), Satan accuses us before God. "The accuser of our brethren has been thrown down, who accuses them before our God day and night" (Rev. 12:10). But before he can accuse, he must first snare a person in sin so that there is a factual basis for his devilish charge.

The idea of the snare is vividly illustrated in the Scriptures. It was the tactic of the Pharisees: "Then the Pharisees went and counseled together how they might trap Him in what He said" (Matt. 22:15). Idolatry snares the soul: "The graven images of their gods you are to burn with fire; you shall not covet the silver or the gold that is on them, nor take it for yourselves, lest you be snared by it, for it is an abomination to the Lord your God" (Deut. 7:25).

Death snares life at an unsuspecting moment: "Moreover, man does not know his time: like fish caught in a treacherous net, and birds trapped in a snare, so the sons of men are ensnared at an evil time when it suddenly falls on them" (Ecc. 9:12, cf. Luke 21:34-35). Money provides an evil snare also: "But those who want to get rich fall into temptation and a snare and many foolish and harmful desires which plunge men into ruin and destruction" (1 Tim. 6:9). Unbelievers can also be caught in Satan's snare (2 Tim. 2:26).

There are two kinds of reproaches. First, there is the reproach for being righteously consistent (Rom. 15:3; Heb. 10:32-33). That's not in view here. Rather we want to consider the reproach for doing unrighteousness after committing oneself to righteousness. Paul's focus here is on the danger done to God's cause in general and a Christian's effectiveness in particular when factual charges of inconsistency and hypocrisy can be laid at the feet of a believer. The reproach of the devil powerfully retards the advance of God's cause— so seriously that it should not be a part of a Christian's life, especially the life of a Christian leader.

How does it happen? Just as it did with the birds and rabbits I preyed on as a child. When one's appetite for sin is strong enough, the bait looks incredibly tantalizing. You may say to yourself, "My life is my own. What I do on church time is one thing, but my own time is another. And besides, if I am caught, it will only affect me." One who thinks this way will eventually act on a fleshly impulse, and Satan will have another victim. No true Christian sets out to shame the cause of Christ, but when caught in a pattern of sin, that will always be the outcome.

OVERCOMING

Hypocrisy deserves a battleship-type salvo. We all deplore the subtle deceit that makes a person's life a lie. Jesus denounced this kind of spiritual playacting. Responding to the Pharisees, He said, "Woe to you, scribes and Pharisees, hypocrites! For you are like whitewashed tombs which on the outside appear beautiful, but inside they are full of dead men's bones and all uncleanness" (Matt. 23:27).

How can we avoid Satan's trap? First, realize that God is on the fifty-yard line of your life. Whether you are in the community, in the church, or by yourself in the country, the Lord is watching (Ps. 139:7-10; Amos 9:2-4). Live your life to please Him (John 8:29; 2 Cor. 5:9).

Second, commit to always living your life according to the absolute standards of Scripture. Then there will be no question as to how you should live. If you are reproached, it will be for righteousness' sake, nor for evildoing. It will validate, not vilify, your faith.

Keep your behavior excellent among the Gentiles, so that in the thing in which they slander you as evildoers, they may on account of your good deeds, as they observe them, glorify God in the day of visitation. (1 Peter 2:12)

Keep a good conscious so that in the thing in which you are slandered, those who revile your good behavior in Christ may be put to shame. (1 Peter 3:16)

Likewise urge the young men to be sensible; in all things show yourself to be an example of good deeds, with purity in doctrine, dignified, sound in speech which is beyond reproach, in order that the opponent may be put to shame, having nothing bad to say about us. (Titus 2:6-8)

Third, avoid the ultimate ploy of isolationism by reminding yourself that no one lives in a vacuum. Everything we do will have an impact on someone else's life. Take King David for instance. What started out as personal pleasure with a glance at another woman (involving only David) ultimately resulted in another's wife being defiled, the death of a husband, the loss of a child, and the distruption of David's reign (2 Sam. 11–12; Pss. 32; 51).

Philip Zimbardo warns of the danger in today's society.

I know of no more potent killer than isolation. There is no more destructive influence on physical and mental health than the isolation of you from me and of us from them. It has been shown to be a central agent in the etiology of depression, paranoia, schizophrenia, rape, suicide, mass murder. . . .

The Devil's strategy for our times is to trivialize human existence in a number of ways: by isolating us from one another while creating the delusion that the reasons are time pressures, work demands, or anxieties created by economic uncertainty; by fostering narcissism and the fierce competition to be No. 1. [7]

Fourth, employ Paul's instructions to slaves in relationship with their masters in your relationship with the Lord: "Let all who are under the yoke as slaves regard their own masters as worthy of all honor so that the name of God and our doctrine may not be spoken against" (1 Tim. 6:1). Do nothing, say nothing, live nothing that could be used by the enemy to discredit Christianity or shame the name of Christ. For to do so will cause God's name to be blasphemed (2 Sam. 12:14), Christ's cause to be temporarily set back, and your participation in God's kingdom advance to be neutralized. "A good name is to be more desired than great riches, favor is better than silver and gold" (Prov. 22:1).

Whether you are a new believer, a faithful worker in the church, or an elder or pastor, you need to hear and heed Paul's warning about Satan's slanderous bent. The devil ruthlessly seeks to discredit Christ and His people at the highest level. Only a genuine, authentic Christian life will cut Satan off at the pass.

Let's all take to heart Paul's thoughts to a group of first-century Christians.

Do all things without grumbling or disputing; that you may prove yourselves to be blameless and innocent, children of God above reproach in the midst of a crooked and perverse generation, among whom you appear as lights in the world. (Phil. 2:14-15)

DEPRESS OR DESTROY THE BELIEVER'S ENTHUSIASM FOR GOD'S WORK

Satan announced that he was going out of business and would offer his tools for sale to whoever would pay the price. At the time of the sale they were all attractively displayed: Malice, Hatred, Envy, Jealousy, Sensuality, and Deceit among them. Each was marked with its own price.

In a far corner lay a harmless-looking, wedge-shaped tool, much worn, and priced higher than any of the others. Someone asked Satan what it was.

"That's Discouragement," he replied.

"Why do you have it priced so high?"

"Because," said the devil, "it is more useful to me than any of the others. I can pry open a man's mind with this when I cannot get him with any of the others."

8. Scheme of Pessimism

"Jessica's OK!" Tears and cheers greeted eighteen-month-old Jessica McClure as she emerged from her fifty-eight-hour ordeal, having fallen twenty-two feet into an eight-inch water well shaft. One newscaster dubbed her "one tough toddler."

This real-life drama quickly captured the attention and emotions of the American public, because the odds were stacked against Jessica. Yet this little girl valiantly fought back to do the impossible—survive. She—and her rescuers—refused to be pessimistic.

Jessica's circumstances picture Satan's desire for us. When we are so far behind the eight ball that recovery seems and feels impossible, the devil would like nothing better than to hear us say, "I quit." When hope departs, then we stand on the edge ready for a spiritual plunge onto the rocks of despair.

SCHEME: PESSIMISM—1 THESSALONIANS 2:14–3:10

SATAN'S LIE: DIFFICULT CIRCUMSTANCES MEAN I WILL NEVER ACCOMPLISH ANYTHING

SIGNIFICANT FOR GOD.

GOD'S TRUTH: 1 CORINTHIANS 15:57-58

If you have not personally identified with Satan's schemes so far, I suspect these coming lies might give you cause for déjà vu. While sharing this material with God's flock at our church, almost everyone raised a hand when I asked, "Within the last three months, how many of you have experienced this kind of devilish attack on your walk with Christ?"

Maybe you've triumphed over Satan's design to distort or deny Scripture. I hope you won't be fooled by the devil's tricks to lure you into a compromising situation that would discredit your Christian testimony. If you've experienced victory over Satan's strategies so far, watch out for this third one.

Wanting you to think contrary to God's Word and to act disobediently to God's will, the devil's third major strategy is to destroy your enthusiasm for God's work. While you might expect Satan to aim at namby-pamby Christian wimps with this strategy, just the opposite is true. The Apostles Peter and Paul served as two of Satan's most frequent targets in the New Testament. These schemes make effective assaults on the souls of spiritual giants.

Satan's plan will be to identify a vulnerable area of your life, such as difficult life circumstances, weak personal qualities, or experiences of spiritual failure. Then, like a good boxer, he will continue to punch at that wound until it becomes so battered, bloodied, painful, and ugly that you drop out of the fight before the end. Paul fought one such battle.

PERSECUTION

The greatest days in Christ's church have been during times of persecution. It's true today in the Soviet Union and China. Tyndale, Hus, Wycliffe, and Bunyan proved it with their martyrdom centuries ago, and Paul points the Thessalonians in this direction also (1 Thes. 2:14-18).

Church history testifies that the blood of the martyrs is the seed of the church.

The prophets, the Lord Jesus, the churches in Judea, Paul and his companions, and the Thessalonians themselves knew intense persecution because they exposed the world's darkness with the light of God's righteousness. Paul writes as a persecuted ambassador of God who is deeply concerned for the young flock at Thessalonica. Like a nursing mother and loving father, he longs to be with them and care for their spiritual needs.

Paul had been torn away from his spiritual children in Thessalonica (Acts 17:5-9). Paul wanted to return, but in his absence, he had not forgotten them. He wanted to go back, but Satan blocked the way (1 Thes. 2:18).

The Greek word translated "thwart" in the *New American Standard Bible* most commonly pictures a military maneuver designed to stop enemy progress. At times timbers were cut and placed on the road to make it impassable, or the road itself was badly damaged. Satan had halted the progress of his enemy Paul toward the Thessalonians.

Paul quickly recognized that Satan lived out the meaning of his name—"adversary." Furthermore, the apostle acknowledged that his adversary was Satan, not just an unfortunate set of circumstances. The right enemy is identified. He's our enemy too.

Persecution marks the normal Christian life (2 Tim. 3:12). Read Hebrews 11:32-40, which chronicles the faith walk of Old Testament saints. Remember that eleven out of the twelve Apostles died as martyrs.

PRAISE

Paul responds to persecution like a thermostat not a thermometer. Instead of merely measuring the temperature of life, he sets it to his desired level. Rather than breaking down in defeat, Paul rises up in celebration.

For who is our hope or joy or crown of exultation? Is it not even you, in the presence of our Lord Jesus at His coming? For you are our glory and joy. (1 Thes. 2:19-20)

Habitually, the apostle looked through to the other side of the storm clouds where he gazed into the glory of God. How did he do it? Paul chose to focus not on himself but rather on God and the flock at Thessalonica (2:19). Paul's "other people" perspective made it all worthwhile. This focus characterized his ministry. His letter to Thessalonica has such phrases as "for all of you" (1:2), "for your sake" (1:5), "a fond affection for you" (2:8), "impart to you . . . our own lives" (2:8), and "you may walk in a manner worthy of . . . God" (2:12). Twice in 2:19-20 he zooms in on "you" not on "me."

Also he set his affections on things above, not below (Col. 3:1-2). Paul was far more interested in God's kingdom advance than in his own personal success. He chose to concentrate on the eternal rather than the temporary.

Undoubtedly, Paul viewed himself as an optimist—one who looked on the brighter side and expected the best. He didn't let Satan, the all-time great promoter of pessimism, lead him to emphasize adverse aspects of life or to expect the worst. Some might have considered Paul a Pollyanna, but he faced reality with the certainty of the Lord Jesus and of a new world coming.

We have at least two motivations to be spiritually optimistic and praise God in the midst of adverse circumstances. First, we have the sure knowledge that in the end Jesus wins. We stand on the victory side of life. Second, we have the optimistic statements of Scripture which say that God can work good out of the worst situations. "And we know that God causes all things to work together for good to those who love God, to those who are called according to His purpose" (Rom. 8:28). "And as for you, you meant evil against me, but

God meant it for good in order to bring about this present result, to preserve many people alive" (Gen. 50:20).

PROXY

Since he was prevented from returning to Thessalonica, Paul sought for another solution (3:1-2). This allowed him not only to keep his focus on God but also to accomplish his purpose, for his chief end was not a personal visit but rather ensuring the personal and spiritual welfare of the flock.

Undoubtedly, Paul and his co-laborers, Silas and Timothy, sought God's wisdom in the matter. They might have prayed, "Lord, what will give You the greatest glory?" or "What solution will be for the greatest advance of Your kingdom cause?" After a time, they thought it best to split up and send Timothy back to the Thessalonians in Paul's place.

I'm sure Paul delighted in the fruit of his discipleship relation with Timothy. It had begun months earlier in Derbe and Lystra (Acts 16:1), and now Timothy would go where Paul could not. This would be Timothy's pattern for many years to come. While he was imprisoned in Rome, Paul sent Timothy on an important mission to Philippi (Phil. 2:19-22). Finally, Paul put his mantle on Timothy's shoulder and charged him to continue the ministry (2 Tim. 4:1-2).

PROTECTION

One man well summarized the two tasks of a shepherd. "The shepherd's task includes both feeding and exhorting. If the sheep are only fed and not exhorted, they are merely being fattened for the slaughter. If they are only exhorted and not fed, they will starve to death." Paul concerned himself with both.

Paul's heart desire was for the glory of God's cause and the good of the Thessalonian church (3:3-4). This Puritan prayer expresses well the allegiance of Paul's heart that helped him to defeat Satan's scheme of pessimism.

Sovereign God,

Thy cause, not my own, engages my heart, and I appeal to Thee with greatest freedom to set up Thy kingdom in every place where Satan reigns;
Glorify Thyself and I shall rejoice, for to bring honour to Thy name is my sole desire.
I adore Thee that Thou art God, and long that others should know it, feel it, and rejoice in it.
O that all men might love and praise Thee, that Thou mightest have all glory from the intelligent world!
Let sinners be brought to Thee for Thy dear name!
To the eye of reason everything respecting the conversion of others is as dark as midnight,
But Thou canst accomplish great things; the cause is Thine, and it is to Thy glory that men should be saved.
Lord, use me as Thou wilt, do with me what Thou wilt; but, O, promote Thy cause, let Thy kingdom come, let Thy blessed interest be advanced in this world! O do Thou bring in great numbers to Jesus! Let me see that glorious day, and give me to grasp for multitudes of souls; let me be willing to die to that end; and while I live let me labour for Thee to the utmost of my strength, spending time profitably in this work, both in health and in weakness.
It is Thy cause and kingdom I long for, not my own. O answer Thou my request!'

PRIZE

Because of God's power and his own bright perspective, Paul did not go down in defeat. Rather, he cherished the prize of knowing that the Thessalonians flourished in their walk with Christ (3:5-8).

The apostle feared that the flock would be tempted by the one who had thwarted his return. He feared that his ministry would have been in vain; he had a healthy respect for the spiritual damage Satan could cause.

But Paul's spirits soared when he heard of their faith and love. His own heart delighted because the Thessalonians returned his love for them.

The real key for us is in the statement, "For this reason, brethren, in all our distress and affliction we were comforted about you through your faith" (1 Thes. 3:7).

Because Paul's battle was for God's cause and his pain was endured for the Thessalonians' good, he could be comforted to know that he had invested profitably. The apostle could see through the smoke screen of life and see how the bad turned out to be good.

May I suggest that when we suffer or get down with little hope of rebounding, it will be when our cause is more important than God's; when our accomplishments overshadow our contributions to God's success, when we want what we want before God gets what He wants. God will not get the victory when you have such attitudes, and neither will you.

Satan uses the self-centered person for his cause, not God's. There is neither real spiritual high in the hollow victory for self nor any good reason why God should intervene when we have ignored Him in the first place. Paul won the prize because he ran the race to win with his eyes fixed on Jesus (1 Cor. 9:24-27; Heb. 12:1-2).

If you are experiencing persecution, suffering, discouragement, or depression, ask yourself two questions.

■ Is God's cause more important than my personal cause?

■ Is other people's good a higher priority than my own good?

These two focuses, God and others, woven together make a strand that is not easily broken when it is tried by life's destructive forces. Your "below-the-surface" dive will be quickly replaced by upward motion propelled by a better and higher focus.

Polycarp, bishop of Smyrna, stood at the stake ready to be martyred. The Roman proconsul gave him two choices: curse the name of Christ and sacrifice to Caesar, or die. He responded, "Eighty and six years have I served Him and He has done me no wrong. How can I blaspheme my King who saved me?"

As they moved to bind Polycarp to the stake, he ordered, "Leave me as I am, for He who gives me power to endure the fire will grant me to remain in the flames unmoved even without the security you will give by the nails."[2]

God and Polycarp won; Satan lost. Paul won too, and rebounded for more than a decade's worth of additional ministry.

PRAYER

Paul gives us a final tip on how to overcome circumstances and remain a spiritual optimist in spite of the immediate rainstorms in our lives. He gave thanks, rejoiced, and prayed (3:9-10). That's how he kept looking up into heaven.

What happens to your joy in time of distress? How frequent is your thanksgiving to God when the heat is up and the shade absent? Do difficult circumstances intensify your prayer life or reduce it?

If you have fallen off the balance beam of life and struggle to regain your position, let me suggest that prayer will help you right yourself more effectively than anything else. Only by seeking God and His recuperative power do you stand a good chance of rebounding. To seek a solution elsewhere is foolish in light of God's resources and love.

Here is the way to begin. This prayer slipped from the lips of Betty Stam who died for Christ's cause on December 7, 1934 in China. She was an optimist's optimist and a victor in the battle with Satan. You can be too!

Lord, I give up my own purposes and plans, all my own desires, hopes, and ambitions and accept Thy will for my life. I give myself, my life, my all, utterly to Thee, to be Thine forever. I hand over to Thy keeping all of my friendships. All the people whom I love are to take second place in my heart. Fill me now and seal me with Thy Spirit. Work out Thy whole will in my life, at any cost, now and forever. To me to live is Christ. Amen.

Thanks be to God, who gives us the victory through our Lord Jesus Christ. Therefore, my beloved brethren, be steadfast, immovable, always abounding in the work of the Lord, knowing that your toil is not in vain in the Lord. (1 Cor. 15:57-58)

9. Scheme of Negativism

"Stinkin' thinkin'."[1] That's what one man calls it. Every one of us has been there. Fanny Crosby could have used her blindness as an excuse, or Joni Eareckson Tada, her paralysis. Just think of the songs, books, and lovely pictures we wouldn't enjoy today if these two great women hadn't allowed God's strength to flow through their weaknesses.

Paul saw himself as a cracked pot (2 Cor. 4:7), certainly not fit to carry the treasure of God's grace to humanity. He knew affliction, perplexity, and persecution. No one would have blamed him had he given up. But instead he recognized that these circumstances were necessary in order that the surpassing greatness of ministry power be of God and not himself. Paul said no to *stinkin' thinkin'* and rejected Satan's call for early retirement. So can you.

SCHEME: NEGATIVISM—2 CORINTHIANS 12:1-10
SATAN'S LIE: WEAKNESS PREVENTS A PERSON FROM BEING EFFECTIVE FOR GOD.
GOD'S TRUTH: PHILIPPIANS 4:13

Everyone imagines Paul as a guy who had it all together.

Beloved by the saints, esteemed by society's elite, reknowned as perhaps the best orator of his day. Right? Wrong!

Physically, Paul was nothing to write home about. A second-century pastor described him as "a man small of stature, with a bald head and crooked legs ... with eyebrows meeting and nose somewhat crooked."[2] He wasn't exactly a candidate for the cover of *GQ*.

The intellectually elite rejected Paul at Athens as nothing more than a religious fanatic who deserved at best a snobbish sneer (Acts 17:32).

Some young Christian wags in Rome thought they could preach circles around the apostle, so while Paul remained imprisoned for his effective preaching, they began a campaign to discredit him (Phil. 1:15-17).

Toward the end of Paul's distinguished missionary career, only Timothy could be described as a colleague of kindred spirit (Phil. 2:20). In his last imprisonment, Luke alone stood with Paul; everyone else deserted him (2 Tim. 4:11, 16).

Missionary work sounds glamorous only to those who have never done it. Listen to Paul describe his "lap of luxury" experiences.

Five times I received from the Jews thirty-nine lashes. Three times I was beaten with rods, once I was stoned, three times I was shipwrecked, a night and a day I have spent in the deep. I have been on frequent journeys, in dangers from rivers, dangers from robbers, dangers from my countrymen, dangers from the Gentiles, dangers in the city, dangers in the wilderness, dangers on the sea, dangers among false brethren; I have been in labor and hardship, through many sleepless nights, in hunger and thirst, often without food, in cold and exposure. Apart from such external things, there is the daily pressure upon me of concern for all the churches. (2 Cor. 11:24-28)

One of the toughest tasks a church faces is choosing a good minister. A member of an official board undergoing this painful process finally lost patience. He had watched the Pastoral Relations Committee reject applicant after applicant for some fault, alleged or otherwise. It was time for a bit of soul-searching on the part of the committee. So he stood up and read a letter purported to be from another applicant.

Gentlemen,

Understanding your pulpit is vacant, I should like to apply for the position. I have many qualifications. I've been a preacher with much success, and also had some success as a writer. Some say I'm a good organizer. I've been a leader most places I've been.

I'm over fifty years of age. I have never preached in one place for more than three years. In some places, I have left town after my work had caused riots and disturbances. I must admit I have been in jail three or four times, but not because of any real wrongdoing. My health is not good, though I still get a great deal done. The churches I have preached in have been small though located in several large cities. I've not got along well with religious leaders in towns where I have preached. In fact, some have threatened me and even attacked me physically. I am not too good at keeping records. I have been known to forget whom I have baptized.

However, if you can use me, I shall do my best for you.

The board member looked over the committee. "Well, what do you think? Shall we call him?"

The good church folks were aghast. "Call an unhealthy, troublemaking, absentminded ex-jailbird? Who signed the application? Who had such colossal nerve?"

The board member eyed them all keenly before he answered. "It's signed, 'the Apostle Paul.'"

SPECIAL PRIVILEGE

Paul wrote 2 Corinthians not so much to commend the flock but rather to correct it. It seems that this greatly gifted church had rebelled against their spiritual father, Paul.

The Corinthians looked at Paul outwardly and concluded, "His letters are weighty and strong, but his personal appearance is unimpressive, and his speech contemptible" (2 Cor. 10:10). They misinterpreted Paul's Christlike meekness as weakness (2 Cor. 10:1). They concluded that Paul lacked the strength and skills to lead their well-endowed church.

The ministry at Corinth had always been tough. By Paul's own admission he had come to their highly immoral city in weakness, fear, and much trembling (1 Cor. 2:3). Paul even had to be reassured by a vision from God with this confidence-building message:

And the Lord said to Paul in the night by a vision, "Do not be afraid any longer, but go on speaking and do not be silent; for I am with you, and no man will attack you in order to harm you, for I have many people in this city." (Acts 18:9-10)

In 2 Corinthians, Paul goes to great lengths to tame these "spiritual adolescents." He even resorts to boasting. It was necessary, however, to rebuke the Corinthians in hopes that they would cease from their own carnal boastings. This discussion started in 2 Corinthians 10 and comes to a conclusion in chapter 12.

For the first time, Paul recounts his special experience with God some fourteen years previous. In verses 1-6 Paul speaks as though he is bragging on behalf of someone else, but verse 7 makes it clear that he is writing of his own experience.

Whether it was a vision or an out-of-body experience, Paul didn't know. What mattered was its reality—God could tend to the details. Paul entered the third heaven or Paradise. By comparing Jesus' promise to the thief (Luke 23:43) and Christ's affirmation to the Ephesian church (Rev. 2:7), we can conclude that Paul entered the presence of God in heaven. His experience seems to be similar to Isaiah's magnificent experience centuries before (Isa. 6:1-5). But whatever Paul saw and heard was so powerful that he could not even speak about it (12:4) or write it out for others to read.

The Corinthians had boasted in themselves and thus missed Paul's wisdom that a man should not think more highly of himself than' he ought to think (Rom. 12:3). They rejected this ancient counsel: "Let another praise you, and not your own mouth; a stranger, and not your own lips" (Prov. 27:2).

Not all boasting, however, finds disfavor with God. Paul also wrote, "But may it never be that I should boast, except in the cross of our Lord Jesus Christ, through which the world has been crucified to me, and I to the world" (Gal. 6:14). Jeremiah sums it up this way:

Thus says the Lord, "Let not a wise man boast of his wisdom, and let not the mighty man boast of his might, let not a rich man boast of his riches; but let him who boasts boast of this, that he understands and knows Me, that I am the Lord who exercises lovingkindness, justice, and righteousness on earth; for I delight in these things," declares the Lord. (Jer. 9:23-24)

Twice Paul reminded the Corinthians of this important truth (1 Cor. 1:31; 2 Cor. 10:17).

Paul's great confidence in life and ministry rested in the fact that God's assessment of him was what counted, not the

Corinthians' (1 Cor. 4:4). He warns them, "For not he who commends himself is approved, but whom the Lord commends" (2 Cor. 10:18).

With tongue in cheek, Paul boasts in God on behalf of a supposed friend (12:5-6). He hopes the Corinthians will learn about their greater foolishness from Paul's lesser "folly."

SEVERE PROBLEM

Paul lets the cat out of the bag in 12:7 when he describes the "two-sided coin" experience that resulted from his adventure in the third heaven, which up to this time he had chosen not to reveal. God would use Satan's messenger to keep Paul from pride. On the other hand, the devil would work to deflate Paul's faith with his sharpened thorn.

What is the thorn? This figure of speech appears four times in the Old Testament (Num. 33:55; Josh. 23:13; Ezek. 28:24; Hosea 2:6). Three times it refers to people and once to life circumstances. Paul's thorn is most commonly identified as a physical problem, since it is "in the flesh." Malaria, epilepsy, headaches, or eye problems have all been suggested.

However, following the Old Testament usage, several other possibilities strongly commend themselves. As in Hosea 2:6, Paul's thorn could have been the adverse circumstances he experienced while serving the Lord (2 Cor. 11:23-28). In view of the majority Old Testament use and the context here, I would identify Paul's thorn in the flesh as people who are (to use our twentieth-century expression) "a thorn in the side" or "a pain in the neck."

Alexander the coppersmith (2 Tim. 4:14), Hymaneaus with Philetus (2 Tim. 2:17-18), and Elymas (called by Paul "son of the devil" in Acts 13:10) all qualify. Let me suggest another possibility—the Corinthians themselves. It's fascinating to note that Paul is coming to the Corinthians for the *third time* (13:1). I rather suspect Paul had prayed on the occasion of each visit, "Lord, spare me the pain."

Satan meant the thorn for evil; God used it for good. Paul won both ways—that's why God never totally relieves our lives of problems. They jolt us back to the reality best expressed by Peter, "Humble yourselves, therefore, under the mighty hand of God, that He may exalt you at the proper time, casting all your anxiety upon Him, because He cares for you" (1 Peter 5:6-7).

SINCERE PETITION

Paul's problems drove him to prayer (12:8). As Jesus prayed three times in Gethsemane, so Paul prayed. He prayed that the thorn—whether physical, circumstances, or people—would be removed. Most likely he saw it only as hindering his ministry. He needed to have a new dimension of understanding added by the Lord, who would use the thorn for Paul's spiritual profit.

God responded, "My grace is sufficient for you, for power is perfected in weakness." What a wonderful truth! We don't need more grace; we just need to rejoice and thank God for the adequacy of His all-sufficient grace. Grace saved us, and it will also sustain us. "He who began a good work in you will perfect it until the day of Christ Jesus" (Phil. 1:6). We start with grace, and we'll finish with grace. God's grace magnificently rules supreme.

God's grace supplements our weakness with God's power. That way no one will doubt God's involvement in our lives, and we won't mistake who should get the glory.

The Corinthians really needed to understand this principle, because they boasted in their own power, which was really weakness.

For consider your calling, brethren, that there were not many wise according to the flesh, not many mighty, not many noble; but God has chosen the foolish things of the world to shame the wise, and God has chosen the weak things of the world to shame the things which are strong, and the base things of the world and the despised, God has chosen, the things that are not, that He might nullify the things that are, that no man should boast before God. (1 Cor. 1:26-29)

In Paul, God had taken a murderer and made him a lifegiver. By Paul's own admission, he was the greatest of sinners (1 Tim. 1:15) and the least among saints (Eph. 3:8); by God's power he became a spiritual giant. He watched with approval from the sidelines as the crowd stoned Stephen (Acts 7:58); years later he would be stoned for preaching like Stephen (Acts 14:19).

Earlier Paul had written, "We have this treasure in earthen vessels, that the surpassing greatness of the power may be of God and not from ourselves" (2 Cor. 4:7). For most people, the affliction, perplexities, persecutions, and beatings Paul experienced would be enough to finish them off for good. But because of God's power graciously perfected in Paul's weakness, Paul became a divinely enabled survivor who was not crushed, did not despair, and was neither forsaken nor destroyed.

Too often we think God will accept our worst or our mediocre efforts and make them good. That's not what Paul is teaching here. Even our best effort is little or nothing in the economy of God's kingdom if God's grace and power aren't co-laborers. The Corinthians did their best in the flesh, compared it to Paul's best in the Spirit, and concluded that Paul was weak and they were strong.

Man's best without God's grace may bring accolades from people, but scorn rains down from God. Philip Edgecomb Hughes put it this way, "The greater the servant's weakness, the more conspicuous is the power of his Master's all-sufficient grace."[3]

SUBLIME PEACE

With God's reassurance, Paul is content (12:10). Instead of struggling internally, he rests, satisfied that God knows best. This wasn't just a momentary victory either. Later on Paul would write this testimony from a Roman prison:

Not that I speak from want; for I have learned to be content in whatever circumstances I am. I know how to get along with humble means, and I also know how to live in prosperity; in any and every circumstance I have learned the secret of being filled and going hungry, both of having abundance and suffering need. I can do all things through Him who strengthens me. (Phil. 4:11-13)

Look carefully at the circumstance in which Paul lives content in Christ. When mean talk comes his way, he will still rest easy. When other people or just life in general gives him a hard time, satisfaction in God's grace rules in his heart. He had taught this to the Corinthians.

No temptation has overtaken you but such as is common to man; and God is faithful, who will not allow you to be tempted beyond what you are able, but with the temptation will provide the way of escape also, that you may be able to endure it. (1 Cor. 10:13)

Now he teaches it again through his own personal practice.

Not for just any cause will Paul live out such a high commitment, only "for Christ's sake." Christ had saved him; now he serves the Saviour. It's no wonder, since Paul at one time was blind but Christ gave him sight (2 Cor. 4:4). He had been dead but now he has life (Eph. 2:1). Who wouldn't serve such a wonderful gift giver? If God can act that powerfully at the point of our greatest weakness, imagine what else He can do if we will walk by faith just as we first believed by faith

(Col. 2:6).

SUMMING UP

Paul's story is not new. Similar stories could be recited by Joseph (Gen. 37–50), Moses (Ex. 2–4), David (1 Sam. 16), and Daniel (Dan. 1–2). But what about you? God's greatest triumphs have arisen in the midst of certain defeats because His power prevailed.

Several great lessons emerge from Paul's experience to encourage and equip us in our battle against Satan's devices.

■ The evil intended by Satan to discourage became instead God's instrument to lift up and empower.

■ Paul prayed for God's will, not his own. When God answered Paul's specific prayer by saying no, Paul knew God had said yes to a better way.

■ Only when our resources are stretched to their limits and we fall short of the goal, exhausted by our best effort, do we become candidates for God's sufficient grace, which is unlimited and inexhaustible.

■ Paul's weakness did not keep God's strength from prevailing.

■ Knowing that God worked through his efforts, even when perceived as puny and frail, Paul rested, knowing that God's will would prevail and God's glory would not fail. The simple truth is that our weaknesses actually qualify us to be effective for God. "I can do all things through Him who strengthens me" (Phil. 4:13).

10. *Scheme of Defeatism*

A dear pastor friend recently wrote these candid comments to me.

I am presently looking for a second job in order to offset the possibility that the church might not be able to pay my salary in the near future. It is the most soul-destroying, wearisome activity I have ever endured. But it has given me a remarkable insight into the financial pressures and discouragements of men who cannot find work or are underemployed.

Please pray for the church and its growth. Please pray for me; Satan regularly overwhelms me with fears and discouragement. And, taking God out of the equation, his fears and discouragements are perfectly logical. I do not know when I last had a full night's sleep without waking up in the midst of one of these satanic attacks. It has worked out for good, however, in that I have learned the value of incessant supplication before God's throne, even though much of that time occurs when I would rather be sleeping.

Defeat delights the devil and fulfills his grandest plan. That's why the fear of failure haunts us all.

SCHEME:	DEFEATISM—LUKE 22:31-34
SATAN'S LIE:	A PERSON WHO HAS FAILED IS NO LONGER USEFUL IN THE KING'S SERVICE.
GOD'S TRUTH:	PSALM 32:1-7

Einstein could not speak until he was four years old and did not read until he was seven. Beethoven's music teacher said about him, "As a composer he is hopeless." When Thomas Edison was a young boy, his teachers said he was so stupid he could never learn anything. When F.W. Woolworth was twenty-one, he got a job in a store but was not allowed to wait on customers because he "didn't have enough sense." Walt Disney was once fired by a newspaper editor because he was thought to have "no good ideas." Caruso was told by one music teacher, "You can't sing. You have no voice at all." An editor told Louisa May Alcott that she was incapable of writing anything that would have popular appeal.

Can you imagine failing twice in business before turning twenty-five? Or having your sweetheart die and experiencing nervous breakdowns at the ages of twenty-six and twenty-seven? Losing eight of ten elections for public office over a period of twenty-five years? For most people, that would cause them to never attempt anything significant again. For Abraham Lincoln, it qualified him to become the sixteenth president of the United States—perhaps our greatest chief executive.

Not everyone rebounds like Lincoln, though. For some, one defeat spells doom for a lifetime, like the commanding officer of a British cruiser who missed a maneuvering signal and turned in the wrong direction. Several near collisions resulted, and the scene could be described as maritime chaos. When some order had been restored, the admiral sent this urgent message to the erring officer, "Captain, what are your intentions?" He immediately replied, "Sir, I plan to buy a farm."[1] He viewed one mistake as irreversible failure.

That's exactly how Satan wanted Peter to view his mistakes. If the devil could have gotten Peter to think, "Once a failure, always a failure," then he would have scored a major victory for the side of darkness.

FOREWARNING

During their last regular meal together, Jesus turned to Peter and told him about a price to be paid for greatness in the kingdom. The disciples had been discussing who among them ranked as the greatest.

"Simon, Simon, behold, Satan has demanded permission to sift you like wheat" (22:31). Satan, not being content with just Judas, was going after the other disciples as well. In the Greek text, *you* is plural, not singular, referring to all the disciples. In a sense, Jesus acknowledges Peter as leader and alerts him to the devil's design for the whole group, as though Peter would be responsible for their recovery.

Satan's sifting would be a brutal experience. Just as men winnowed wheat with short, violent shakings to separate the fruit from the chaff, so would Satan attempt to jerk the disciples loose from their faith in Christ and His kingdom.

Jesus then spoke even more specifically. "I tell you, Peter, the cock will not crow today until you have denied three times that you know Me" (22:34). Failure stares Peter square in the face. Satan will clutch Peter, like a wild animal would a rag doll, and shake him violently until he's about to come apart at the seams.

It's no wonder Peter would later write, "Be of sober spirit, be on the alert. Your adversary, the devil, prowls about like a roaring lion, seeking someone to devour" (1 Peter 5:8). He reports this truth having once been the bait on which Satan chewed. We need to avoid underestimating the devil's power and ability and intently be on the lookout. We need to understand that as God granted permission for Satan to touch spiritual giants like Job and Peter, so He will us. Christian, to be forewarned is to be forearmed. Be on the lookout, for Satan's prowl is real.

If I could ask Peter how to combat Satan's attack, he would probably answer like this:

> But resist him, firm in your faith, knowing that the same experiences of suffering are being accomplished by your brethren who are in the world. And after you have suffered for a little while, the God of all grace, who called you to His eternal glory in Christ, will Himself perfect, confirm, strengthen and establish you. (1 Peter 5:9-10)

FOOLHARDINESS
"No way, Jose!" That would be our knee-jerk response to Christ's warning. And likewise Peter replied, "Lord, with You I am ready to go both to prison and to death!" (22:33) Peter's commitment ran deep, to the core. He just didn't realize how severely it would be tried.

Peter's naiveté showed. He thought his side was on the brink of winning the war when in fact boot camp wasn't even over yet. He sounded like an adolescent who sincerely but foolishly boasts of tackling the world. He doesn't yet realize that instead of conquering, Christ will be crucified. Instead of being welcomed as a liberator, Christ will be opposed as the enemy.

It's not that Jesus didn't warn them. Or that Peter didn't take the condition of discipleship seriously. Christ's words, like these, must have flashed through his mind.

> If anyone comes to Me, and does not hate his own

115

*father and mother and wife and children and brothers
and sisters, yes, and even his own life, he cannot be My
disciple. Whoever does not carry his own cross and
come after Me cannot be My disciple. (Luke 14:26-27)*

But talking about fighting the battle is miles from actually
engaging in combat. An ancient soldier wisely advised, "Wait
to brag until you remove the armor, rather than boast as you
put it on." Peter would have been well advised to hold his
tongue until later. And so would we.

But before we get too tough on Peter, I believe Peter's
boast was sincere. Later on, in fact, he did go to prison (Acts
4:3; 5:18; 12:3-4) for Christ's cause. In the end he did die for
his faith—like his Saviour by crucifixion, only upside down,
according to historical tradition.

I grow leery when I hear people publicly say what they're
willing to do for Christ. It's all I can do to refrain from asking,
"Have you considered the price?" Too many want to steal
second base and still keep a foot on first, to use a baseball
analogy. You can't do it! Risk for Christ's sake is basic to
spiritual victory. And that's scary stuff.

May I suggest that instead of blurting out a young warrior's
boast, we check in with a seasoned soldier of another era to
see how he prepared for the war. David prayed,

*Search me, O God, and know my heart; try me and
know my anxious thoughts; and see if there be any
hurtful way in me, and lead me in the everlasting way.
(Ps. 139:23-24)*

FALTERING
Jesus indicated that Peter would not fail unrecoverably, but
that he would falter (Luke 22:32). It's inevitable, and it's also
certain to be our experience in this life too.

When Smart People Fail jumped off the shelf at me while

I browsed through a favorite bookstore. It contains an insightful discussion of the subject. The authors list nine major reasons why people fail.

1. *Poor interpersonal skills*
2. *Round peg in a square hole situation*
3. *Lack of commitment*
4. *Uncontrollable circumstances*
5. *Self-destructive behavior*
6. *Scattered efforts*
7. *Prejudice*
8. *Poor management*
9. *Overstaying our welcome*[2]

In Peter's case, reason 4 prevailed. Circumstances he could not control invaded his life. It's good to know that God promised, "The steps of a man are established by the Lord; and He delights in his way. When he falls, he shall not be hurled headlong; because the Lord is the One who holds his hand" (Ps. 37:23-24). My advice to us all is to hold tight to our Heavenly Father's hand.

Jesus had prayed that Peter's stumble would not end in irreversible failure. "I have prayed for you, that your faith may not fail" (22:32). How would you feel if Jesus prayed for you? Encouraged? He did pray for you, soon after He prayed for Peter.

"I do not ask in behalf of these alone, but for those also who believe in Me through their words" (John 17:20). Christ also now stands at the right hand of the Father acting as our advocate (1 John 2:1), no doubt defending us against the accusations of Satan (Rev. 12:10).

Peter's test would be tough and swift. Survival meant success and it would equip him to strengthen the other disciples (22:32). Peter's experience not only fell short of being fatal, but prepared him for spiritual fulfillment.

FULFILLMENT

Months ago one of our staff wrote me this note, which alerted me again to Satan's ways.

I especially identify with Moses and appreciated your perspective of him. Most have seen him as lazy and/or rebellious in his decline initially to lead Israel—but I have perceived him to be depressed and dealing with very real feelings of inadequacy. Satan so effectively uses our failures to defeat us again and again.

Samson recovered (Jud. 16:28-30). So did David (Ps. 51) and John Mark (2 Tim. 4:11). Peter joins their ranks, and so can you. They show us the way.

After Peter denied Christ three times he went out and wept bitterly (Luke 22:62). What would you do? He was on the ropes and could easily have climbed out of the ring and walked away forever. But somehow a sense of God's love, His mercy, and grace must have stirred Peter, because several days later he's back in the fight.

The eleven reassembled after Christ's crucifixion and the women reported to them Christ's resurrection (Luke 24:10-11). Peter, along with John, raced to the tomb to see if this could be true (24:12). Peter had faced up to his fall and thus could join the disciples again. Undoubtedly, he admitted his ill-advised attitude and out-of-character behavior. The disciples openly welcomed him back, not only because of his honest admission, but because they knew from Christ's words that Satan had set him up.

Peter was there when Christ appeared later on that night as the disciples met behind locked doors (Luke 24:36-43). Peter could face the Saviour because he had turned his back on his denial, admitted it, and returned as Christ had instructed him. The marvel of Peter's experience rests not in his fall but in his recovery and return to true fellowship with Christ. Peter stands forever as your model if ever you have stumbled. Peter shouts out, "Come home, child of God."

Later on Christ restored Peter to ministry. It happened in Galilee. In the midst of a seaside breakfast, Jesus told Peter, "Tend My lambs. . . . Shepherd My sheep. . . . Tend My sheep" (John 21:15-17). What joy must have filled Peter's soul as the Master reaffirmed His trust in Peter and his ability to minister!

As Paul's thorn had two sides, one for Satan and another for God, so did Peter's sifting. He is now prepared to understand God's power, which sustained him in the battle, and Satan's fury, which nearly destroyed his ministry. It's not surprising then that on the Day of Pentecost Peter steps out as God's chief spokesman. We're not shocked to see Peter as the dominant figure in Acts 1–12. God's Spirit had reenergized him for the building of Christ's church. Peter experienced victory in Jesus.

FINAL THOUGHTS

The way of recovery points us to God's mercy and forgiveness. It rests not in us but in Him, even though we must admit our detours, lapses, letdowns, and sins. Satan's lie is that there is no life after the agonizing bitterness of defeat. God's truth reflects just the opposite. Listen to David, a recovering failure.

How blessed is he whose transgression is forgiven, whose sin is covered! How blessed is the man to whom the Lord does not impute iniquity, and in whose spirit there is no deceit! When I kept silent about my sin, my body wasted away through my groaning all day long. For day and night Thy hand was heavy upon me; my vitality was drained away as with the fever heat of summer. I acknowledged my sin to Thee, and my iniquity I did not hide; I said, "I will confess my transgres-

sions to the Lord"; and Thou didst forgive the guilt of my sin. Therefore, let everyone who is godly pray to Thee in a time when Thou mayest be found; surely in a flood of great waters they shall not reach him. Thou art my hiding place; Thou dost preserve me from trouble; Thou dost surround me with songs of deliverance. (Ps. 32:1-7)

Why not follow Peter and David's lead, if you today walk the path on which they traveled centuries ago? Repent of your faltering ways, return to the comfort and strength of your gracious God, and ask Him to restore you and reenergize your walk with Christ.

When you do, like Peter, you'll be better equipped to champion the cause of Christ. You will have more compassion on those who are down, because you have been there. You'll be purer, because the dross of sin has been burned off by the fires of trial. Strength will be yours in greater ways, because your life has been tempered by the white hot flame of testing. New levels of commitment will be reached, because your confidence in God has ascended even higher.

The initial year in my very first senior pastorate proved exceedingly difficult at best. When those months of agony turned into relieved history, my kids gave me a T-shirt that read, "Dad survived his first year at Grace." By God's grace, in spite of Satan's repeated attacks and my own naiveté, I could shout with exhilaration, "I've lived to minister another day for God's glory." Praise God for his sustaining hand of love.

All of you who share the experience of waging spiritual warfare can identify with this "rough rider" of another generation, Theodore Roosevelt.

The credit belongs to the man who is actually in the arena, whose face is marred by dust and sweat and blood; who strives valiantly; who errs and comes short again and again, who knows the great enthusiasms, the great devotions, and spends himself in a worthy cause; who at the best, knows the triumph of high achievement; and who, at the worst, if he fails, at least fails while daring greatly, so that his place shall never be with those cold and timid souls who know neither victory nor defeat.[3]

O B J E C T I V E **4**

DILUTE THE EFFECTIVENESS OF GOD'S CHURCH

Millions of Christians live in a sentimental haze of vague piety, soft organ music, trembling in the lovely light from stained glass windows. Their religion is a thing of pleasant emotional quivers, divorced from the real, divorced from the intellect, and demanding little except lip service to a few harmless platitudes. I suspect that Satan has called off the attempt to convert people to agnosticism. If a man travels far enough away from Christianity he is always in danger of seeing it in perspective, and deciding that it is true. It is much safer, from Satan's point of view, to vaccinate a man with a mild dose of Christianity, so as to protect him from the real thing.

William Culbertson

11. Scheme of Cultism

Jonestown. In November 1978 Jim Jones led his People's Temple to the ultimate cult experience—following their leader in death. More than 900 people, including children, died at Jones' jungle compound in Guyana. They all drank poisoned Kool-Aid.

Not all cults end as tragically nor can they all be identified as easily. Some disguise themselves so well that even Christians are fooled. While cults differ in many ways and defy formulaic descriptions, they all share a common characteristic—a wrong view of salvation.

SCHEME: CULTISM—LUKE 22:3-6
SATAN'S LIE: SALVATION IS BASED ON WORKS RATHER THAN ON FAITH ALONE IN JESUS CHRIST.
GOD'S TRUTH: EPHESIANS 2:8-10

One of Long Beach, California's premier tourist attractions is the H-4 Hercules, better known as the Spruce Goose. People pay big money just to look at it today, decades after its first and last flight on November 2, 1947. Its wings span 320 feet, and from nose to tail it measures 219 feet. This eight-engine, 213-ton flying behemoth cost $40 million to build. What did it accomplish? Just one flight of less than 1,000 yards at an altitude that never exceeded 70 feet.[1] Satan would love for us to build "Spruce Goose" type churches that are memorialized in record books but do little or nothing to advance God's kingdom.

Charles Swindoll comments on a fascinating machine that I once saw at the Smithsonian Institute in Washington, D.C.

> *Many a church is like an impressive machine I once read about. It had hundreds of wheels, cogs, gears, pulleys, belts, and lights, which all moved or lit up at the touch of a button. When someone asked, "What does it do?" the inventor replied, "Oh, it doesn't do anything—but doesn't it run beautifully?"*[2]

It's beautiful to behold, designed with precision engineering, and efficient beyond imagination. But what does it do? Nothing productive! That's the kind of church Satan wants Christians to build.

God designed the church to be fruitful. He set down realistic, measurable goals in the Great Commission (Matt. 28:18-20). Satan's fourth major "mind game" objective for believers calls for Christians being extremely active, expending lots of energy, building magnificent buildings and programs, spending huge sums of money, talking a lot about God, and setting new records. Yet when the dust has settled and the question is asked, "What did you accomplish?" the answer comes back, "Not much in regard to the Great Commission." That's Satan's plan to dilute God's church.

PROBLEM

Since the beginning, Satan has tried to sidetrack God's plan of salvation. By Herod's hand he tried to murder Christ in the city of His birth (Matt. 2:16). The devil himself attempted to solicit Christ's allegiance by worship in return for an "instant" kingdom (Matt. 4:8-9).

Through Peter, Satan tried to talk Christ out of going to the cross (Matt. 16:21-23). In Judas, Satan sold out Christ's cause for a mere thirty shekels of silver.

> And Satan entered into Judas who was called Iscariot, belonging to the number of the twelve. And he went away and discussed with the chief priests and officers how he might betray Him to them. And they were delighted, and agreed to give him money. And he consented, and began seeking a good opportunity to betray Him to them apart from the multitude. (Luke 22:3-6)

Through the ages, Satan has had his ambassadors. Paul called them false apostles and deceitful worshipers (2 Cor. 11:13-14). They, like their leader, Satan, disguise themselves as angels of light and servants of righteousness. The apostle writes of these men and his fear for the Corinthians.

> But I am afraid, lest as the serpent deceived Eve by his craftiness, your minds should be led astray from the simplicity and purity of devotion to Christ. For if one comes and preaches another Jesus whom we have not preached, or you receive a different spirit which you have not received, or a different gospel which you have not accepted, you bear this beautifully. (2 Cor. 11:3-4)

Paul's concern needs to be reechoed in our own day. Our world is awash with the counterfeit.

PROTOTYPE

Judas Iscariot models the most deceitful form of counterfeit Christian leadership ever in human history. He becomes the mold from which all other wolves in sheeps' clothing come. He tricked everyone to the very end, except Jesus, who knew from the first that Judas would fulfill an Old Testament prophecy in the life of Messiah (John 13:18; Ps. 41:9).

As far as we know, Judas was the only non-Galilean disciple. In all probability, he came from the Judean village of Kerioth from which comes the identifying name Iscariot, which in Hebrew means "man of Kerioth." He must have been a man of some training and abilities, for he was placed in charge of the money (John 13:29). It becomes evident that early on Judas found more interest in money than in ministry. He pilfered the money (John 12:6) and finally sold out altogether for thirty pieces of silver.

Amazingly, in light of his end, Judas heard all of Christ's teaching for he was included among the twelve. He would have cast out demons and healed the sick along with the other eleven (Matt. 10:1). Jesus might have had Judas in mind when he warned,

> Not every one who says to Me, "Lord, Lord," will enter the kingdom of heaven; but he who does the will of My Father who is in heaven. Many will say to Me on that day, "Lord, Lord, did we not prophesy in Your name, and in Your name cast out demons, and in Your name perform many miracles?" And then I will declare to them, "I never knew you; depart from Me, you who practice lawlessness." (Matt. 7:21-23)

Undoubtedly Judas entered into the discussions on who would be greatest in the kingdom (Luke 22:24). He, like the rest, believed the kingdom would come immediately (Luke 19:11) and he would reap a rich reward as a high-ranking official in return for the few first years of poverty and uncertainty.

I personally believe Judas far outdistanced his uneducated

colleagues in intelligence, quickness of mind, and cunning-ness. Judas tried to cultivate Christ's favor by works and not by faith. His motive was his own gain, not the furtherance of Christ's cause. He was a master at buttering up the boss and appearing to do good even while plotting to do evil.

And [Jesus] answered and said, "He who dipped his hand with Me in the bowl is the one who will betray Me. The Son of Man is to go, just as it is written of Him; but woe to that man through whom the Son of Man is betrayed! It would have been good for that man if he had not been born." And Judas, who was betraying Him, answered and said, "Surely it is not I, Rabbi?" He said to him, "You have said it yourself." (Matt. 26:23-25)

Although Scripture does not tell us, the best guess as to why Judas defected is that he, first of all the disciples, real-ized that Jesus really would die, and there was not to be an immediate political kingdom from which Judas could profit in reputation and power. Judas plotted to minimize his losses by getting out quick and starting afresh with a few shekels.

Because Christ had a price on his head and because Ju-das' heart yearned for money, he sold Christ out.

Then one of the Twelve, named Judas Iscariot, went to the chief priests, and said, "What are you willing to give me to deliver Him up to you?" And they weighed out to him thirty pieces of silver. And from then on he began looking for a good opportunity to betray Him. (Matt. 26:14-16)

Judas did the ultimate when he betrayed Christ with a kiss (Matt. 26:48-49). That which had the appearance of affection raged with the alienation of an assassin. Thus Judas earned the title "son of perdition" (John 17:12). He became a tool in the hand of Satan. Praise God, who turned Judas' evil into good through Christ's death and resurrection.

PATTERN

Thousands of Judases have come and gone since the first century. More confusion reigns today than ever before as the counterfeits have multiplied at an alarming rate. I'm often asked by new Christians, "How can I tell the genuine from the counterfeit?"

Cults do have a pattern. There are some marks which brand so-called Christian groups cultic. Not every cult will be characterized by all of these marks, but they will embrace many. Use these qualities to judge a religious organization.

Financial exploitation. Rather than appealing to God's grace as the motive for giving, cults require members to give certain percentages or amounts. As much time is devoted to money as to ministry. In the more bizarre cases, members are asked to deed over their entire portfolio to the organization. Members become slaves to the cult and must depend totally on the organization for everything.

Scattered Bible teaching. They'll focus on a few Bible truths rather than consider the whole counsel of God. Frequently they give more attention to the teachings of their leaders than to Scripture. They ride their cultic hobbyhorses constantly.

Minimizing, distorting, or denying the deity of Jesus Christ. In spite of Scripture's clear teaching, they insist on a Jesus who is not fully God. They use clever ploys and word games to circumvent the direct teaching of Scripture.

Mysterious inside information. You cannot understand their teachings without their help. Unless you understand their own special rules, which only they know, you can never make sense of truth. You become a doctrinal slave to their system, and honest questions or inquiry receive the cold shoulder.

Denunciation of all other religious organizations. Cults promote themselves as the exclusive holders of truth. They refuse to recognize that no one religious organization has an exclusive claim to the truth.

Flexible doctrines. At times there will be dramatic alterations in their teachings because of a particular situation. They desperately attempt to hide these changes from historical inquiries.

Authoritarian leadership. The cult leaders claim (directly or indirectly) supposed messianic credentials as a basis of authority. They tend to demand absolute obedience. The cult leader rests on the pedestal of deity. Few members will question this once inside the cult's web of influence.

Belief in sacred texts other than the Bible. Frequently other books supersede or interpret Scripture. The Bible takes a back seat to more recent "revelation," which usually comes from the cult's founder or leader.

Salvation by works. They may teach salvation by faith *plus works*, but in every instance they add human achievement to God's divine accomplishment in the Lord Jesus Christ. This stands as the ultimate mark of a counterfeit Christianity. They pervert the wonderful grace of God and the free gift of salvation through Jesus' death and resurrection.

Legitimate Christian churches and organizations can take on some of these characteristics, particularly those near the top of my list. I've used this list to check out my own ministry and that of our church to make sure we are not being suckered by Satan and set up to be ineffective.

PERVERSION
The early church had not celebrated too many birthdays before perversion reared its ugly head. Paul warned of assaults from the outside and subversion from within (Acts 20:29-30). Until Jesus returns, the danger will escalate.

Two perversions concern us here: claims of salvation

through *a person other than Jesus Christ* and claims of salvation through *a way other than faith alone by God's grace.*

Salvation by *another person* or *another way* fools few people who are familiar with Christian doctrine. A little more confusing is salvation by *another person* but the *right way.* Most confusing, even to genuine Christians, is salvation through the *right person* but the *wrong way.* We are so do-it-yourself oriented that adding our works to God's work does not offend, even though the clear teaching of Scripture is that salvation is through faith alone.

True salvation comes only through *the right person* and *the right way,* only through Jesus Christ and only by faith. Judas looked for a while at the *right person,* but he pursued the *wrong way* and thus ended up bound for hell.

Warnings about assaults on the Gospel fill the pages of our New Testament. See for example Jude 3-4; Galatians 1:6-9; 2 Corinthians 11:2-4; 2 John 7-11; and Rev. 3:15-17. If the scheme of cultism prevailed so intensely in the first generation after Christ, imagine how dominant it could be today. The only way to stunt its growth and halt its advance is the way of truth. Only a return to the unvarnished truth of the pure Gospel will stave off this danger.

That's why Peter wrote,

Therefore, I shall always be ready to remind you of these things, even though you already know them, and have been established in the truth which is present with you. And I consider it right, as long as I am in this earthly dwelling, to stir you up by way of reminder, knowing that the laying aside of my earthly dwelling is imminent, as also our Lord Jesus Christ has made clear to me. And I will also be diligent that at any time after my departure you may be able to call these things to mind. (2 Peter 1:12-15)

PROTECTION

The most valuable and eternally significant piece of information rests in the answer to the question, "What must I do to inherit eternal life?" That's what the Gospel is all about. The Gospel answers that most important of all questions. We cannot be reminded of its content too often.

The Gospel is presented throughout Scripture in different words and phrases, but every passage says the same thing: salvation is by God's grace through faith in the Lord Jesus Christ, who died for our sins and rose from the grave to grant eternal life to those who believe in Him.

Read without interruption these descriptions of the Gospel from several different passages of Scripture.

But as many as received Him, to them He gave the right to become children of God, even to those who believe in His name, who were born not of blood, nor of the will of the flesh, nor of the will of man, but of God. (John 1:12-13)

For God so loved the world, that He gave His only begotten Son, that whoever believes in Him should not perish, but have eternal life. (John 3:16)

And there is salvation in no one else; for there is no other name under heaven that has been given among men, by which we must be saved. (Acts 4:12)

If you confess with your mouth Jesus as Lord, and believe in your heart that God raised Him from the dead, you shall be saved; for with the heart man believes, resulting in righteousness, and with the mouth he confesses, resulting in salvation. For the Scripture says, "Whoever believes in Him will not be disappointed." For there is no distinction between Jew and Greek; for the same Lord is Lord of all, abounding in riches for all who call upon Him; for "Whoever will call upon the name of the Lord will be saved." (Rom. 10:9-13)

Now I make known to you, brethren, the gospel which I preached to you, which also you received, in which also you stand, by which also you are saved, if you hold fast the word which I preached to you, unless you believed in vain. For I delivered to you as of first importance what I also received, that Christ died for our sins according to the Scriptures. (1 Cor. 15:1-3)

For by grace you have been saved through faith; and that not of yourselves, it is the gift of God; not as a result of works, that no one should boast. For we are His workmanship, created in Christ Jesus for good works, which God prepared beforehand, that we should walk in them. (Eph. 2:8-10)

He saved us, not on the basis of deeds which we have done in righteousness, but according to His mercy, by the washing of regeneration and renewing by the Holy Spirit, whom He poured out upon us richly through Jesus Christ our Saviour. (Titus 3:5-6)

The true Gospel focuses on the *right person*—Jesus Christ. The true Gospel teaches the *right way*—through faith by God's grace. Death is something we earn by sinning, but salvation is received as a free gift. "For the wages of sin is death, but the free gift of God is eternal life in Christ Jesus our Lord" (Rom. 6:23).

PRACTICALITY

How will our lives be affected if we successfully sidestep the scheme of cultism? First, we'll redouble our efforts to communicate the true Gospel. We'll go out of our way to make sure people know that Jesus said, "I am the way, and the truth, and the life; no one comes to the Father, but through Me" (John 14:6). There is only one way. Our proclamation will clarify that salvation comes by faith alone in the crucified and resurrected Saviour.

This word is not for preachers or teachers only. All Christians should share their faith. Every believer should be looking for opportunities to tell others how God can change their lives. This is an all-hands alert to share the right Gospel.

Second, we must be sure we believe the right Gospel. To believe in the wrong person or to pursue heaven on a pathway other than faith leads to eternal death not life. We need to ensure that we have believed in the true Gospel.

Third, for the sake of coming generations, we must perserve the genuine Gospel. Like Jude of old, we must contend earnestly for the faith which was once for all delivered to the saints (Jude 3). If we don't, we'll build elaborate church machines that do nothing and fly nowhere, like the Spruce Goose.

12. *Scheme of Egoism*

When I became the pastor of my present church, a dear woman sent a card to welcome me and to share an important spiritual truth. Her message was, "Brother, don't ever try to be a big preacher. Instead, preach a big Saviour." I'm thankful to her for that special encouragement to watch out for pride, which has claimed so many in ministry (1 Tim. 3:6).

Of pride, C.S. Lewis writes, "There is no fault which makes a man more unpopular, and no fault which we are more unconscious of in ourselves. And the more we have it ourselves, the more we dislike it in others."[1]

Let's all admit that we have a pride problem. No one is immune. Then let's search together through the life of David to find out why he became unpopular with God and how he recovered. What worked for David will also work for us.

SCHEME: EGOISM—1 CHRONICLES 21:1-17
SATAN'S LIE: WHAT PEOPLE ARE OR ACHIEVE IS DUE TO THEIR OWN ABILITIES RATHER THAN GOD'S ACTIVITY IN THEIR LIVES.

GOD'S TRUTH: 1 PETER 5:6

One dictionary defines *egoism* as "a doctrine that individual self-interest is the valid end of all interests."[2] Pride puts self-interest above the interests of God and others. Egoism is haughty arrogance that sees life revolving around the self, and it epitomizes an anti-God state of mind. It is the opposite of love, which does not brag, is not arrogant, and does not seek its own (1 Cor. 13:4-5).

A friend of mine told me of a humorous incident that occurred when he served as a new ensign aboard a destroyer in the South China Sea. The fleet was operating in formation late at night when a radio signal ordered a change for all ships. As each moved to new stations his crew observed that their destroyer and an aircraft carrier were on a collision course. Unable to remedy the situation on their own, the inexperienced sailors called for the captain, who was sleeping in his sea cabin. Still half asleep, he ran out onto the bridge to assess the problem. Confused by all the moving ships and in a state of panic, he screamed at my frightened friend, "Where are we?" My friend answered, "R-R-Right in the m-middle of the r-r-radar scope, Sir!" Little did he realize that every ship in the United States Navy is in the center of its own radar scope.

That's the essential mark of *egoism*—living life as though we are in the center of everything. If your life doesn't revolve around God and others, then watch carefully as David demonstrates the disaster that will follow.

DIABOLICAL PROBE

"Then Satan stood up against Israel and moved David to number Israel" (1 Chron. 21:1). David's latter years lacked the glory and successes of his youth. He sinned in his involvement with Uriah and Bathsheba (2 Sam. 11–12). Then came the conflict between Amnon and Absalom (2 Sam. 13), followed by Absalom's revolt and the eviction of his own father from the throne and capital city (2 Sam. 14–18). To top it all off, Sheba instituted a public slander campaign against the king (2 Sam. 20).

Now David encounters Satan. Johann Wolfgang von Goethe wrote this right-on line in *Faust,* "The devil is an egotist" (Act I, scene i). Remember that Satan said,

> *I will ascend to heaven; I will raise my throne above the stars of God, and I will sit on the mount of assembly in the recesses of the north. I will ascend above the heights of the clouds; I will make myself like the Most High. (Isa. 14:13-14)*

Satan desires to win as many to his side as possible. When he's successful, the plan of God temporarily takes a detour.

Scripture clearly teaches that pride doesn't please God. The first in a list of seven deadly sins is "haughty eyes" (Prov. 6:16-17). "Everyone who is proud in heart is an abomination to the Lord; assuredly, he will not be unpunished" (Prov. 16:5). Both James and Peter (quoting Prov. 3:34) warn the New Testament church, "God is opposed to the proud, but gives grace to the humble" (James 4:6; 1 Peter 5:5). Satan suckered David into the arena of self, and from there it was certain disaster for Israel.

DIVINE PROVOCATION

Second Samuel 24 records the parallel passage to 1 Chronicles 21. "Now again the anger of the Lord burned against Israel, and it incited David against them to say, 'Go, number Israel and Judah.' " This sounds so different from 1 Chronicles 21!

While doing a nationally broadcast Bible Q & A program, a caller asked me, "Doesn't the Bible contradict itself at 1 Chronicles 21 and 2 Samuel 24? In one place it says God moved David and in the other it says Satan moved him." I pointed her to three passages—the story of Job, Judas' betrayal of the Lord, and Paul's thorn. In each of these we saw the drama of God and Satan interacting over the same person. Satan can do nothing without God's permission. Where freedom is granted to Satan, God will work out good and righteousness from what Satan intends to be evil.

Neither 1 Chronicles 21 nor 2 Samuel 24 gives the events leading up to this point. It would appear that the nation was pressuring David to number the fighting men in a census, very possibly because of a strong military threat. At some point, Satan encouraged David to do it and God, wanting to teach Israel and David a lesson, allowed it to happen by giving God's people over to the desire of their hearts.

DAVID'S PRIDE

The king called for Joab, his nephew and the general of David's army. "Go, number Israel from Beersheba even to Dan, and bring me word that I may know their number" (1 Chron. 21:2). David yielded to the pressure of the situation, the push of the people, and Satan's relentless pounding.

God later brought severe punishment on the nation for this decision. But why? Some have suggested that David did not collect the tax required for a census as outlined in the Mosaic Law (Ex. 30:12). Others speculate that David did it so he could brag about the size of his army, and it is true that he had come a long way since the days of his ragtag band of 400 (1 Sam. 22:2).

Another possibility is that David believed his success came more from his ability than from God's faithfulness to keep His promises to Israel. Maybe David felt he could take greater confidence in the size of his army than in the size of his God. This seems most likely, in light of the pressure from the people. Two of the finest Old Testament scholars ever to write note, "The true kernel of David's sin was to be found, no doubt, in self-exaltation, inasmuch as he sought for the strength and glory of his kingdom in the number of the people and their readiness for war."[3]

Hezekiah would later walk this same pathway. God miraculously delivered him from the hand of Sennacherib and 185,000 Assyrian soldiers in one night without even a battle (Isa. 37:36). Then later Hezekiah sold out to the Assyrians and tried to mediate peace by human means, not divine intervention (2 Kings 20:12-19). The commentary on this event reads, "But Hezekiah gave no return for the benefit he received, because his heart was proud; therefore wrath came on him and on Judah and Jerusalem" (2 Chron. 32:25).

Better would it have been for both David and Hezekiah to have taken the way of Jehoshaphat who prayed, "O Lord, the God of our fathers, art Thou not God in the heavens? And art Thou not ruler over all the kingdoms of the nations? Power and might are in Thy hand so that no one can stand against Thee" (2 Chron. 20:6). Then he listened to the prophet Jahaziel who proclaimed, "Listen, all Judah and the inhabitants of Jerusalem and King Jehoshaphat: thus says the Lord to you, 'Do not fear or be dismayed because of this great multitude, for the battle is not yours but God's'" (2 Chron. 20:15).

DESIGNED PREVENTATIVES

Joab responded to David's request, "May the Lord add to His people a hundred times as many as they are! But, my lord the king, are they not all my lord's servants? Why does my lord seek this thing? Why should he be a cause of guilt to Israel?" (1 Chron. 21:3). Joab strongly opposed the census, but the will of the king prevailed.

David bypassed two preventatives designed by God to avoid just such a disaster as would come on Israel. First, David ran right past God's principle of seeking multiple counsel. "Where there is no guidance, the people fall, but in abundance of counselors there is victory" (Prov. 11:14). "For by wise guidance you will wage war, and in abundance of counselors there is victory" (Prov. 24:6).

Had David listened to Joab and sought other godly counsel from his elders, he probably would not have numbered the people. By rejecting the time-honored divine wisdom of multiple counsel, David embarked on the inevitable road to tragedy.

Second, David failed to take God's advice in the Psalms. Perhaps he authored these words himself: "The king is not saved by a mighty army; a warrior is not delivered by great strength. A horse is a false hope for victory; nor does it deliver anyone by its great strength" (Ps. 33:16-17).

David sinfully put his trust in himself and his army, not in God, who had delivered him so many times before. This is where Satan won the victory, and egoism dominated David's thinking.

DIRECT PENITENCE

David's heart troubled him after he received Joab's census report (2 Sam. 24:10). After a fitful night with little sleep, the king realized that he had greatly sinned against God (1 Chron. 21:8). So he asked for forgiveness just as he had done earlier in his life (Pss. 32 and 51).

To David's credit, he realized and acknowledged his wrong. He did the only right thing and threw himself on the mercy of God. "But now, please take away the iniquity of Thy servant, for I have done very foolishly" (21:8).

Note that David understood his responsibility for his sin. He didn't blame the people for their pressure nor Satan for his involvement.

He didn't try to make Joab the scapegoat. Rather, as a man after God's own heart (Acts 13:22), David openly confessed his sin and asked for God's forgiveness. Although God did forgive him, David's sin was not without consequences that stagger the imagination.

DIVINE PUNISHMENT

Instead of striking only David, God poured His wrath out on Israel. David could have withheld God's wrath had he withstood the pressure of his people to act in an ungodly way. But now, after the fact, all he could do was reduce the punishment's intensity.

God offered David three punishments from which to choose. They were three years of famine, three months of military defeat, or three days of the sword of the Lord (1 Chron. 21:9-12).

David answered, "I am in great distress; please let me fall into the hand of the Lord, for His mercies are very great. But do not let me fall into the hand of man" (1 Chron. 21:13). The king understood that to fall into the hand of man economically through famine or militarily through invasion would be to experience ruthless cruelty. He preferred to rest in the hands of the merciful God.

The result? The Lord sent a pestilence, and 70,000 people died. Can you imagine the death toll had God not been merciful? That surely helps us understand the awfulness of sin and the terrible price to be paid to satisfy God's wrath.

Let me ask you, which is the greater sin—adultery or egoism? Think about it! In David's case of adultery only two persons died—Uriah and the child (2 Sam. 11:15, 17; 12:14, 18). In David's bout with pride, 70,000 people died. The abomination of pride in God's sight is great.

David's true heart shows through clearly in the midst of this divinely inflicted trauma. He and his elders (whom he neglected to consult previously) publicly repented and David pleaded with God,

Is it not I who commanded to count the people? Indeed, I am the one who has sinned and done very wickedly, but these sheep, what have they done? O Lord my God, please let Thy hand be against me and my father's

household, but not against Thy people that they should be plagued. (1 Chron. 21:17)

This is a strong reminder to me of my responsibility as a pastor, husband, and father. What horrible consequences may come to my charges if I fall prey to Satan's assaults on my spiritual leadership.

DAILY PRACTICE

Psalms 130 and 131 seem to express David's response to these dark days of his kingship. First, there is the song of forgiveness:

Out of the depths I have cried to Thee, O Lord. Lord, hear my voice! Let Thine ears be attentive to the voice of my supplications. If Thou, Lord, shouldst mark iniquities, O Lord, who could stand? But there is forgiveness with Thee, that Thou mayest be feared. (Ps. 130:1-4)

Then David affirms his commitment to humility:

O Lord, my heart is not proud, nor my eyes haughty; nor do I involve myself in great matters, or in things too difficult for me. Surely I have composed and quieted my soul; like a weaned child rests against his mother, my soul is like a weaned child within me. O Israel, hope in the Lord from this time forth and forever. (Ps. 131)

Every Christian should memorize this antidote to Satan's poisonous pride. "Humble yourselves, therefore, under the mighty hand of God, that He may exalt you at the proper time" (1 Peter 5:6). As Christ humbled Himself by being obedient to death on the cross, so should we humble ourselves under the mighty hand of God; and as God exalted Christ, so will He exalt us at the proper time (Phil. 2:9). We are to walk in the humble ways of our Lord Jesus Christ. True humility will be marked by these qualities.

■ A greater desire to serve than to be lord (Matt. 20:26-27).

■ Peace in being last rather than first (Matt. 20:16).

■ Contentment in living low instead of high (Phil. 4:11-12).

■ More satisfaction in giving than receiving (Acts 20:35).

■ A compulsion to forgive rather than to exact punishment (Matt. 18:21-35).

■ A desire for exaltation only by the hand of God (Matt. 23:12).

These qualities marked the One who walked this earth as the model of humility—the Lord Jesus Christ. Let's be like Him. "Blessed are the gentle, for they shall inherit the earth" (Matt. 5:5).

13. *Scheme of Antagonism*

"Seven—seven—zero—zero . . . I have an emergency. Gun-fire." Two minutes later PSA flight 1771 fell out of the sky and violently impacted a hillside near San Luis Obispo. All forty-three people aboard died.

Quick work by the FBI and FAA identified the gunman as a former employee, fired from his job weeks earlier. Friends said he "harbored a hair-trigger temper and an unpredictable streak of violence." In venting his anger at the supervisor who fired him and the airline that released him, this man carried his temper to the ultimate—mass murder.

Anger, however, is not new to the human race having been with us from almost the beginning. Cain and Abel, sons of Adam and Eve, brought offerings to the Lord. Abel's sacrifice pleased God, but Cain's displeased the Lord. When Cain discovered this, he became exceedingly angry and in a volatile outburst murdered his brother in history's first recorded homicide (Gen. 4:1-8).

The Bible says Satan, who was a murderer from the begin-ning, promotes unhealthy anger (John 8:44). But God gives us a solution to tame our temper.

SCHEME: ANTAGONISM—EPHESIANS 4:26-27
SATAN'S LIE: IT IS HEALTHY TO REGULARLY VENT ANGER AT OTHER PEOPLE.
GOD'S TRUTH: JAMES 1:19-20

Dr. Albert Rothenberg, an associate professor of psychiatry at Yale University School of Medicine, said this to his fellow therapists about our anger-plagued society.

> *As clinicians we devote a considerable portion of our thinking and practice to unearthing, clarifying and tracing the permutations of anger in our patients. In depression we look for evidence of anger behind the saddened aspect; in hysteria we experience angry seductiveness; in homosexuality and sexual disorders, we see angry dependency; in marital problems we unearth distorted patterns of communication particularly with respect to anger; we interpret the presence of anger, we confront anger, we draw anger, we tranquilize anger and we help the working through anger.[1]*

He recognized the centrality of anger to many contemporary problems.

I recently read about the book *Anger: The Misunderstood Emotion* written by Carol Tavris, a social psychologist who has made the study of anger her special field. Her conclusions came as a complete surprise to her colleagues and created tremendous turmoil because they were completely opposite what psychologists have been telling us for the past two decades. Tavris wrote, "The research on the subject indicates that expressing rage has no intrinsic value. In fact, ventilating anger doesn't rid you of the feelings behind it. Anger breeds more anger!"

> *The idea that anger is a natural thing and that its expression is healthy is very American. And it is truly*

narcissistic. . . . There is a saying among the Eskimos that anyone with reason is expected to control his anger except sled dogs, children and Americans. Suppressed hostility isn't such a bad thing after all. It used to be common courtesy. Sometimes the best thing to do about anger is nothing at all. Let it go, and half the time, keeping quiet gives you time to cool down and decide whether the matter is worth discussing or not.[2]

Doesn't that sound remarkably similar to James 1:19-20? Be quick to hear, be slow to speak, and be slow to anger. James did not say that we are never to be angry, but we are to have long fuses. There should be a long time between the match being struck and when the explosive inside me is ignited.

RIGHTEOUS ANGER

Anger is a deed of the flesh, according to Paul (Gal. 5:19-20; Col. 3:8). Our anger is not usually prompted by the Spirit of God, but by our flesh, because we think we haven't gotten our fair shake from life. Somehow our experience hasn't matched our expectation, and we spew the fury of our wrath over those around us.

In the Sermon on the Mount Jesus taught that if you are angry with your brother then you, not he, are deserving of judgment (Matt. 5:22). As a matter of fact, He said if you have something against your brother—if you do not have a clear relationship with another person—don't try to worship God. Your anger creates a barrier between you and God. Make it right with that person and then go worship God.

In Ephesians 4:26-27, the first two words are "Be angry." Some of you have claimed this as your life verse. But you can't do that; you must read in context. "Be angry, and yet do not sin; do not let the sun go down on your anger, and do not give the devil an opportunity."

Paul, by command, says be angry, but then he warns not

to sin in so doing. Satan, our adversary, looks for opportunities to turn supposedly "justifiable" anger into sin. The Bible—and our daily newspapers—are filled with illustrations of this.

Right reasons. As we search the Scriptures, we find that righteous anger can have only one motive—an affront to God. Anger is never a right response when someone has wronged you personally.

Look at our Lord. He was angry, but He was angry only when God was blasphemed. He cleansed the temple twice— once at the beginning of His ministry and again at the end (John 2:14-17; Mark 11:15-17). In both cases He cried out to the religious leaders of the day, "You have made My Father's house a den of thieves." They were an affront to God; therefore, He was angry.

If anger is generally not the right response, it raises the question, "What should I do if somebody sins against me?" The fact is that we as believers are going to sin against each other. When we come to know Christ we're not made perfect. We are transformed, so that we are perfectable over a period of time as we grow in Christlikeness. This process will be completed when God catches us up into heaven, glorifies us, and we remain in His presence forever.

Matthew 18:15 lays out the proper response. If someone sins against you, go to that person and lovingly tell him or her of the wrong. The text says, "If he listens to you, you have won your brother."

God has a process and procedure. Remember, the only right reason for right anger is when an affront is given to God.

Right degree. The only right kind of anger is slow in coming. In God's economy, anger is the last resort, not the first impulse. This basic principle is found in both the Old and New Testaments. "He who is slow to anger is better than the mighty, and he who rules his spirit, than he who captures a city" (Prov. 16:32).

Physicians tell us that one of the causes of coronary problems is constant or repeated outbursts of anger. Many other diseases of the body can also be aggravated by this emotion. Just a few seconds of anger can leave you drained, shaken, or ruined for the rest of the day.

There is an even more important reason to be slow to anger. God is slow to anger, and we are to be like God. The little phrase "slow to anger" is used of God nine times in the Old Testament. In Exodus 34:6, the Lord described Himself to Moses as "compassionate and gracious, slow to anger and abounding in loving-kindness and truth." The same thought is repeated in Numbers 14:18 when the Lord declared, "The Lord is slow to anger and abundant in loving-kindness, forgiving iniquity and transgressions."

Christian, the thing that should strip you of your anger the quickest is the fact that God could have righteously poured out His wrath on you because of sin, yet He chose to be patient and merciful. As God has been to us, so God would have us be to others—extending that same grace even when we have been wronged.

Right way. There is a right way to express our anger. "Tremble and do not sin" (Ps. 4:4). Our anger is to be expressed internally, *not* externally. How does your body feel when you're very angry? One common response is shaking. Your body is completely captured by the anger, and it trembles.

The world tells us to vent that anger in order to stop shaking. God tells us, "Tremble and do not sin." How do I do that? I do it by meditating in my heart; being stilled by offering the sacrifice of righteousness and trusting the Lord.

It is often said that if you don't let your anger out, it will eat you up from the inside out. But that is not true if you deal with it correctly. God wants us to neutralize our anger by being still, thinking about Him, and offering the sacrifices of righteousness. Hebrews 13:15-16 can help you discover the sacrifices of praise and thanksgiving for what God has given.

Proverbs 29:11 tells us, "A fool always loses his temper." It's easy to lose your temper. If your goal in life is to always lose your temper, you can be incredibly successful. But you won't find favor in God's sight. The second half of that verse continues, "but a wise man holds back." Venting anger does not solve the problem. It may provide a temporary release from the pressure inside you, but it does not get rid of the anger.

Right time. The right time is very simple. "Do not let the sun go down on your anger" (Eph. 4:26).

Anger is not something to wallow in for days, weeks, months, and years. It is to be experienced for less than a day. You're never to go to sleep on your anger. Do you know why? If you go to sleep angry, you wake angrier. Your subconscience will feed on that anger and inflame it all night long. Make sure that you've made peace with God in your heart.

What happens if we violate this principle? Doctors variously estimate that 60 to 90 percent of the people in hospitals today are there from emotionally induced illnesses. Wrong emotions expressed over a long period of time will result in physiological and psychological turmoil.

I'll never forget reading an article that explained the tragic death of a number of men. There was a man at a certain workplace who was a pretty placid, easygoing guy. But he came to that point in life where sometimes his experience didn't match expectations. He thought he should have been promoted; instead some of his fellow employees were promoted beyond him. His wife said at that moment he became a changed man.

He was angry. That anger festered inside for two and a half years until he was completely poisoned. One day, Mr. Nice Guy walked into his place of employment with a shotgun; he killed four employees and permanently paralyzed another. Because he carried his anger to the ultimate extreme of murder, today four men are not with their families and another is paralyzed. The angry man's own family has been fractured, and he lives with the remorse of guilt under a lifetime sentence in prison—all because he couldn't cope with anger.[3]

RESISTING ANGER

How can we cope with and control our anger? How can we deal with anger in a godly, Christian way? If you have an anger problem, you need to admit it and do something about it. I want to give you some simple, workable steps that will help you to cope with your anger.

1. Admit that anger is a sin if it is expressed wrongly. James 4:17 says, "Therefore, to one who knows the right thing to do, and does not do it, to him it is sin." If you have an anger problem, it is a sin and needs to be confessed. Don't blame your anger problem on your heredity or temperament. Don't say that it is unconquerable or an absolutely necessary part of your life. Simply agree with God that you have sinned.

2. Confess that sin before God. As a Christian, you've been forgiven through His Son, Jesus Christ. But you've not yet been perfected. So what happens when you sin? That's what 1 John 1:9 is all about. "If we confess our sins, He is faithful and righteous to forgive us our sins and to cleanse us from all unrighteousness."

What happens in a family when children disobey? Parents don't boot them out of the family; they deal with the issue. They talk together, have the kids acknowledge their wrongs, and restore the parent-child relationship.

So it is in the family of God. When you do wrong, God does not yank your salvation card and make you earn it all over again. When you're born into God's family, it is forever.

God gave you salvation by His grace, and He will sustain you by His grace because the blood of Jesus Christ has covered all your sins. But there does need to be that parental transaction between the Father and His spiritual son or daughter.

3. Pray for God to remove that impulse to antagonism from you. First John 5:14-15 tells us,

And this is the confidence which we have before Him, that, if we ask anything according to His will, He hears us. And if we know that He hears us in whatever we ask, we know that we have the requests which we have asked from Him.

However, don't expect God to wave a magic wand and make your anger immediately disappear. It will be a process. You were not made perfect at the moment of salvation, and you will not be made angerless at that moment of prayer. Be willing and eager to change.

4. Feed on the Word of God. Fill your mind with appropriate passages that deal with anger; then look at those verses that deal with peace. I say this because it is a well-known fact that in order to completely break an old habit, you must replace it with a good habit. As you get rid of your anger, you need to replace it with peace.

5. Don't give up. Don't quit. It may be one step forward and eighteen steps backward; then two forward and fifteen backward; then one forward and one back. By God's grace, He'll give us the needed forward motion.

Let me give you tip that I learned from the space program. The astronauts who walked on the moon didn't get there and say, "Boy, I wonder if I can do it?" The scientists learned as much as they could about the moon and simulated it here on earth. The astronauts simulated walking on the moon thousands of times. They checked their equipment, tried different scenarios, and found solutions for anticipated problems. When they actually arrived on the moon, they had confidence that they knew everything they would need to know.

One answer to an anger problem is rehearsing scenarios and the solutions weeks, days, and hours before you get into the heat of battle. When you enter that circumstance, your mind will immediately be flooded with verses on anger or peace, and you will know how to respond.

If you're filled with an uncontrollable rage be prepared to say, "My friend, I'm about to sin. I'm going to turn my back and walk away—not as an affront to you, but so I won't sin against you and God with my anger." Train yourself to walk away and cool off. When you are under control go back and deal with the issue (Prov. 15:1).

I want everyone to understand that I am not saying you should ignore the problem. On the other hand, you can't reach a solution when you are feeling the white-hot, burning passion of anger. Make sure that you are calm, under control, and seeking God's glory, not your own vindication.

6. Find a trusted friend to tell about your problem, and ask that person to pray with and for you. Choose someone who will love you in spite of your problem, someone who will be honest and loving enough to confront you if you start to move backward instead of forward. Make yourself accountable to this friend on a regular basis—weekly or biweekly. Be honest enough to share your defeats as well as your victories. Your friend will encourage you or tell you to get your show in order depending on how well you did.

You will be making yourself very vulnerable, so pick your friend carefully. He or she should be the kind of friend who "walks in when the rest of the world walks out."

7. Read a good book on anger. One of the best books on the subject is *Anger Is a Choice* by Tim LaHaye and Bob Phillips.[4] Chapter 13, "How to Deal with Your Anger," contains many practical hints on how to get a handle on your anger.

Those of you who don't know the bondage of anger won't understand all that I've said. Those of you who are angry people do know the pain, anguish, embarrassment, and problems anger causes in interpersonal relationships. It prevents you from living in peace with yourself and God. I pray for all of us that we will be known as peacemakers, because we have made peace with God and have been able to make peace in the world. "Blessed are the peacemakers, for they shall be called sons of God" (Matt. 5:9).

VICTORY IN JESUS

Question 102 of the historic Westminster Shorter Catechism makes this inquiry about Christ's model prayer (Matt. 6:9-13): "What do we pray for in the second petition?" The answer follows:

In the second petition, which is, "Thy kingdom come," we pray that Satan's kingdom may be destroyed, and that the Kingdom of grace may be advanced, ourselves and others brought into it, and kept in it, and that the Kingdom of glory may be hastened.

Jesus taught His disciples to pray for God's kingdom, which would spell doom for Satan. I can commend no better approach for us. As we pray, we can be confident that the God of peace will soon crush Satan under our feet (Rom. 16:20). But until then, we can defend ourselves.

GOD'S ARSENAL
The great reformer Martin Luther, while translating the New Testament into German at Wartburg Castle, fancied that he

155

saw the prince of darkness prowling about like a lion. So alarmed was Luther that he snatched up his inkstand and flung it at the imagined head of his enemy.

The kingdom has not yet come in the fullness of its glory, and so Satan still roams about to destroy. We need to continue praying, "Thy kingdom come." But in the meantime, believers must rally against Satan, not with an inkstand, but with the faith of children.

When a little girl was asked if Satan ever tempted her to do wrong, she replied, "Oh, yes, the devil does try to get me. But when he knocks at the door of my heart, I just pray, 'Jesus, please go to the door for me!'" "What happens then?" continued her questioner. "Oh, everything turns out all right. When Satan sees Jesus, he runs away every time!"

That is great wisdom from the mouth of a child. We alone are no match for the devil. But our Lord Jesus Christ has not left us defenseless. Let me show you the arsenal that is at our command.

- The Saviour's victory at Calvary (John 12:31, Rev. 12:11).
- The promise of overcoming (1 John 5:4-5; Rev. 21:7).
- The intercessory ministry of Christ (John 17:15, 20).
- The knowledge of Satan's tactics (2 Cor. 2:11).
- The believer's spiritual armor (Eph. 6:10-17).
- The Holy Spirit's indwelling power (1 John 4:4).
- The believer's prayers (Matt. 6:13; Eph. 6:18-20; Mark 9:29).
- The instructions for defeating Satan (James 4:7-8).
- The sure knowledge that Satan has been rendered powerless with regard to death (Heb. 2:14).
- The encouragement of ultimate victory (Rev. 20:1-10).

A SELF-ANALYSIS

If you were Satan and you knew as much about yourself as you do now, what area of your life would you attack to detour yourself from the path of God's will? Since Satan is real and his attack on us is certain, the smartest move we can make is to prepare for the battle. This exercise is designed to help you anticipate the most likely targets of Satan.

There are a number of key areas to include in your thinking. Any of these areas make strategic sites for Satan's mischief: doctrinal convictions; thought patterns and attitudes; physical and material well-being; emotional stability; personal holiness; commitment to obedience; priorities; living by faith; relationships at home; involvement in the local church. List your weak and strong areas in the space provided.

WEAK AREAS   *STRONG AREAS*

Now ask yourself these key questions:
- Where has Satan attacked you in the past?

■ Where has Satan penetrated your defenses in the past?

■ Where is Satan currently active in your life?

Satan is likely to attack the weak areas in your life. On the other hand, he might surprise you with a sneak attack where you least expect it—an area of strength that has been neglected because of complacency.

You can use these questions to help you shore up your defense:

■ What area of your life has been proven weak by past failure?

■ What areas do you suspect are weak as indicated by Satan's frequent temptation?

■ What areas are "blind spots" in your life?

■ What strong areas are you likely to ignore out of pride?

■ What strong areas have you neglected (and thus weakened) due to complacency?

■ In what areas have you recently fought a successful battle and have assumed Satan would not attack there soon again?

After you've completed this self-analysis, rest in the ancient motto *a Deo victoria,* or "God gives the victory." I'm asking God that this prayer would be answered for all of us who dare to challenge Satan's schemes in the power of His Word and His Son Jesus Christ.

A Christian's Prayer

O Lord,
I bless thee that the issue of the battle between thyself and Satan has never been uncertain, and will end in victory.

Calvary broke the dragon's head, and I contend with a vanquished foe, who with all his subtlety and strength has already been overcome.

When I feel the serpent at my heel may I remember him whose heel was bruised, but who, when bruised, broke the devil's head.

My soul with inward joy extols the mighty conqueror.

Heal me of any wounds received in the great conflict; if I have gathered defilement, if my faith has suffered damage, if my hope is less than bright, if my love is not fervent, if some creature-comfort occupies my heart, if my soul sinks under pressure of the fight.

O thou whose every promise is balm, every touch life, draw near to thy weary warrior, refresh me, that I may rise again to wage the strife, and never tire until my enemy is trodden down.

Give me such fellowship with thee that I may defy Satan, unbelief, the flesh, the world, with delight that comes not from a creature, and which a creature cannot mar.

Give me a draught of the eternal fountain that lieth in thy immutable, everlasting love and decree.

Then shall my hand never weaken, my feet never stumble, my sword never rest, my shield never rust, my helmet never shatter, my breastplate never fall, as my strength rests in the power of thy might.'

N O T E S

INTRODUCTION

1. Paul Harvey, *Pulpit Helps*, 7:5, February 1982.
2. Thomas Brooks, *Precious Remedies Against Satan's Devices* (The Banner of Truth Trust, reprinted n.d.), pp. 15–16.
3. C.S. Lewis, *The Screwtape Letters* in *The Best of C.S. Lewis* (Christianity Today, Inc., 1969), p. 13.
4. This study is not intended to cover the work of demons. However, it's assumed that the demonic army of hell helps the devil to carry out his schemes. For a thorough study of demons consult C. Fred Dickason, *Angels: Elect and Evil* (Moody Press, 1975) and *Demon Possession and the Christian* (Moody Press, 1987).

CHAPTER ONE—SATAN'S BATTLE PLAN

1. "The Enemy," (Western Airlines, n.d.).
2. Kenneth Woodward with David Gates, "Giving the Devil His Due," *Newsweek* (August 30, 1982), p. 74.
3. Anton Szandor LaVey, *The Satanic Bible* (Avon Books, 1969), p. 25.
4. Paul Lee Tan, *Encyclopedia of 7700 Illustrations* (Assurance Publishers, 1979), pp. 1234–1235.

CHAPTER TWO—SENSATIONALISM

1. The Greek construction "If you are . . . " could also be translated "Since you are . . . "
2. Flavius Josephus, *Antiquities of the Jews*, Book XV, Chapter xi, Paragraph v.
3. John Bunyan, *Pilgrim's Progress* (Moody Press, reprinted n.d.), p. 46.

CHAPTER THREE—ECUMENICISM
1. Daniel Defoe, "When He Reigns, It's Hell," in *ENDTIME: The Doomsday Catalog,* ed. by William Griffin (Collier Books, 1979), p. 104.
2. Ignatius, "To the Philadelphians," in *The Apostolic Fathers* (Baker Book House, reprinted 1976), p. 80.
3. Elon Foster, *New Cyclopaedia of Illustrations,* Vol. I (1871), p. 189.
4. F.B. Proctor, *Treasury of Quotations on Religious Subjects* (Kregel Publications, reprinted 1977), p. 577.
5. Walter Martin, *The Kingdom of the Cults* (Bethany Fellowship, 1965) and *The World's Great Religions,* 3 Vol. (Time, Inc., 1963).
6. "Ecumenical," in *Webster's Seventh New Collegiate Dictionary* (G. & C. Merriam & Co., 1963), p. 263.

CHAPTER FOUR—RATIONALISM
1. See Richard Mayhue, "Eve: A Long-shot Loser" in *A Christian's Survival Guide* (Victor Books, 1987), pp. 36–47, for a look at Satan's attempt to lure Eve with the scheme of materialism as the other major distorting attack recorded in Scripture.
2. This is one way *Webster's Ninth New Collegiate Dictionary* (Merriam-Webster, Inc., 1984) defines *rationalize.*

CHAPTER FIVE—SITUATIONALISM
1. Paul Tan, *Encyclopedia of 7700 Illustrations* (Assurance Publishers, 1979), p. 561.
2. Thomas Watson, *A Body of Divinity* (The Banner of Truth Trust, reprinted 1978), p. 132.
3. Charles Colson, *Grace Today* (September 1987), p. 12.
4. Paul Tan, *Encyclopedia,* p. 560.

CHAPTER SIX—INDIVIDUALISM
1. Because of the context of immorality in 1 Corinthians 6–7 and because celibacy is certainly no sure cure against immorality, I believe the NIV translation errs in its interpretive translation of 7:1, "Now for the matters you wrote about: It is good for a man not to marry."
2. Ella Wheeler Wilcox, "An Unfaithful Wife to Her Husband," quoted in J. Allan Petersen, *The Myth of the Greener Grass* (Tyndale House Publishers, 1984), pp. 59–61.

CHAPTER SEVEN—ISOLATIONISM
1. "Why the Secrets Slip Out," *U.S News and World Report* (June 1, 1987), p. 20.
2. Timothy D. Schellhardt. "What Bosses Think About Corporate Ethics," *The Wall Street Journal* (April 6, 1988), p. 27.
3. Paul Robbin, "A Study in Paradox," *Leadership* (Winter 1980), p. 118.

NOTES

4. Sinclair Ferguson, "Where God Looks First," *Eternity* (February 1987), p. 34.

5. "Integrity" in *Webster's Ninth New Collegiate Dictionary* (Merriam-Webster, Inc., 1984), p. 628.

6. Joseph Ryan, "Wanted: People of Integrity," *Discipleship Journal* (31:1985), p. 18.

7. Quoted by Charles R. Swindoll, *Seasons of Life* (Multnomah Press, 1983), p. 337.

CHAPTER EIGHT—PESSIMISM

1. Arthur Bennett, ed., *The Valley of Vision* (The Banner of Truth Trust, 1975), p. 177.

2. William Barclay, *The Revelation of John,* Vol. I (The Westminster Press, 1976), pp. 76–77.

CHAPTER NINE—NEGATIVISM

1. Zig Ziglar, *See You at the Top* (Pelican Publishing Co., 1978), p. 32.

2. Richard Longenecker, *The Ministry and Message of Paul* (Zondervan Publishing House, 1971), p. 23.

3. Philip E. Hughes, *Commentary on the Second Epistle to the Corinthians* (Wm. B. Eerdmans Publishing Co., 1962), p. 451.

CHAPTER TEN—DEFEATISM

1. Gary Inrig, *Hearts of Iron, Feet of Clay* (Moody Press, 1979), p. 254.

2. Carole Hyatt and Linda Gottlieb, *When Smart People Fail* (Simon & Schuster, 1987), pp. 103–130.

3. Theodore Roosevelt, quoted in *Commitment to Excellence* (Graphicenter, Inc., 1984), p. 76.

CHAPTER ELEVEN—CULTISM

1. Alan Russell, ed., *1987 Guinness Book of World Records* (Bantam Books, 1987), pp. 315–316.

2. Charles R. Swindoll, *Hand Me Another Brick* (Thomas Nelson Publishers, 1978), p. 141.

CHAPTER TWELVE—EGOISM

1. C.S. Lewis, "Christian Behavior" in *The Best of C.S. Lewis* (Christianity Today, Inc., 1969), p. 497.

2. *Webster's Ninth New Collegiate Dictionary* (Merriam-Webster, Inc., 1984), p. 398.

3. C.F. Keil and F. Delitzch, *Commentary on the Old Testament,* Vol. II (Wm. B. Eerdmans Publishing Co., n.d.), p. 502.

CHAPTER THIRTEEN—ANTAGONISM

1. Vernon Grounds, *Emotional Problems and the Gospel* (Zondervan

Publishing Co., 1976), pp. 51–52.

2. Tricia Crane, "Why Is This Woman Smiling?" in the *Daily News,* Section NE (March 7, 1983), pp. 1–2.

3. Tim LaHaye, *How to Win Over Depression* (Zondervan Publishing Co., 1974), p. 91.

4. Tim LaHaye and Bob Phillips, *Anger Is a Choice* (Zondervan Publishing Co., 1982).

AFTERWORD—VICTORY IN JESUS

1. Arthur Bennett, ed., *The Valley of Vision* (The Banner of Truth Trust, 1975), p. 181.

HELPFUL READING

Barnhouse, Donald G. *The Invisible War.* Zondervan Publishing House.

Bounds, E.M. *Satan: His Personality, Power and Overthrow.* Baker Book House.

Breese, Dave. *Satan's Ten Most Believable Lies.* Moody Press.

Brooks, Thomas. *Precious Remedies against Satan's Devices.* The Banner of Truth Trust.

Dickason, C. Fred. *Angels: Elect and Evil.* Moody Press.

Dickason, C. Fred. *Demon Possession and the Christian.* Moody Press.

Guiness, Os. *The Gravedigger File.* InterVarsity Press.

Lewis, C.S. *The Screwtape Letters.* Macmillan Co.

Lockyer, Herbert. *Satan: His Person and Power*. Word Books.

Morgan, G. Campbell. *The Voice of the Devil*. Baker Book House.

Pentecost, J. Dwight.. *Your Adversary the Devil*. Zondervan Publishing House.

Sanders, J. Oswald. *Satan Is No Myth*. Moody Press.

Tatford, Frederick A. *Satan: The Prince of Darkness*. Kregel Publications.

Wiersbe, Warren. *The Strategy of Satan*. Tyndale House Publishers.